Women in Education

Patricia Cayo Sexton

WOMEN
IN
EDUCATION
By
Patricia Sexton

PHI DELTA KAPPA
Educational Foundation
Bloomington, Indiana

Perspectives in American Education

This book is one of a five-volume set published by Phi Delta Kappa as part of its national bicentennial year program.
The other titles in the set are:

The Purposes of Education, by Stephen K. Bailey
Values in Education, by Max Lerner
Alternatives in Education, by Vernon Smith, Robert Barr, and Daniel Burke
Melting of the Ethnics: Education of the Immigrants, 1880-1914, by Mark Krug

Introduction

The two hundredth anniversary of the American declaration of separation from the government of England has stimulated millions of words of sentiment, analysis, nostalgia, and expectation. Much of this verbal and pictorial outpouring has been a kind of patriotic breastbeating. Most of it has been rhetoric.

Several years ago the leadership of Phi Delta Kappa announced its determination to offer a significant contribution to the bicentennial celebration in a series of authoritative statements about major facets of American education that would deserve the attention of serious scholars in education, serve the needs of neophytes in the profession, and survive as an important permanent contribution to the educational literature.

The Board of Directors and staff of Phi Delta Kappa, the Board of Governors of the Phi Delta Kappa Educational Foundation, and the Project '76 Implementation Committee all made important contributions to the creation of the Bicentennial Activities Program, of which this set of books is only one of seven notable projects. The entire program has been made possible by the loyal contributions of dedicated Kappans who volunteered as Minutemen, Patriots, and Bell Ringers according to the size of their donations and by the support of the Educational Foundation, based on the generous bequest of George Reavis. The purpose of the Foundation, as stated at its inception, is to contribute to a better understanding of the educative process and the relation of education to human welfare. These five volumes should serve that purpose well.

A number of persons should be recognized for their contributions to the success of this enterprise. The Board of Governors of the Foundation, under the leadership of Gordon Swanson, persevered in the early planning stages to insure that the effort would be made. Other members of the board during this period were Edgar Dale, Bessie Gabbard, Arliss Roaden, Howard Soule, Bill Turney, and Ted Gordon, now deceased.

The Project '76 Implementation Committee, which wrestled successfully with the myriad details of planning, financing, and publicizing the five activities, included David Clark, Jack Frymier, James Walden, Forbis Jordan, and Ted Gordon.

The Board of Directors of Phi Delta Kappa, 1976 to 1978, include President Bill L. Turney, President-Elect Gerald Leischuck, Vice Presidents William K. Poston, Rex K. Reckewey, and Ray Tobiason and District Representatives Gerald L. Berry, Jerome G. Kopp, James York, Cecil K. Phillips, Don Park, Philip G. Meissner, and Carrel Anderson.

The major contributors to this set of five perspectives on American education are of course the authors. They have found time in busy professional schedules to produce substantial and memorable manuscripts, both scholarly and readable. They have things to say about education that are worth saying, and they have said them well. They have made a genuine contribution to the literature, helping to make a fitting contribution to the celebration of two hundred years of national freedom. More importantly, they have articulated ideas so basic to the maintenance of that freedom that they should be read and heeded as valued guidelines for the years ahead, hopefully at least another two hundred.

—Lowell Rose
Executive Secretary,
Phi Delta Kappa

Contents

Women and Schools

The Functions of Education
for Women

While sex bias has certainly strained the relationship between women and schools, through the years the relationship has generally been harmonious and of considerable mutual benefit. Women have supported the schools and been among their chief allies. In turn the schools have, with some prodding, helped women to grow, perform their family roles, and find a place for themselves outside the home.

This close relationship is based on certain similarities in the functioning of two social institutions, the family and the primary school. A traditional function of women in the family has been the nurture and instruction of the young. A similar function has been taken over by the schools, beginning in the nursery school and stretching out even into secondary education. During the early years of child rearing they offer women some relief from the strains of child-rearing tasks. While women of means once hired tutors, nurses, nannies, baby-sitters to help them raise their children, they now simply send them off to school.

As children grow older the situation begins to change. The closer students come to the transition from school to job—in higher education, professional schools, vocational education—the less likely is the partnership to work well for women.

The process of sorting and selecting students in

preparation for jobs begins in earnest. Schools start to match students with their traditional adult roles. They segregate them into different courses of study and different schools, opening doors to some and closing them to others. As this process advances, the serious effects of sex discrimination are felt and the relationship between women and schools becomes most strained. In higher education especially, where students are selected for the most choice jobs in the society, the effects of sex discrimination in male-dominated work institutions are felt most acutely.

The schools have served women in various ways. They have stood *in loco parentis* and helped women and their child-rearing tasks. As employers, they have provided many desirable jobs for women. In offering role models to the young, they have supplied many living examples of successful career women, the teachers themselves. In their role as interpreter of an ostensibly democratic and meritocratic ideology, they have taught the value of equal opportunity and, in the early school years at least, they have treated females perhaps more equitably than have other social institutions.

In these roles, elementary and secondary schools have helped to raise the consciousness, aspirations, and expectations of women. They have also helped to lower some of the barriers to equal opportunity that exist in the larger society.

Because of these benefits, women have been among the leading advocates of free public education through the years, much as they are now advocates of publicly sponsored day-care programs. Without schools to care for their children during working hours, young mothers would have found it far more difficult to fill new roles outside the home and move toward greater personal autonomy.

In their *in loco parentis* role, schools have become mother substitutes for at least part of the day. Standing in place of parents, they have reduced the work burden of housewives and the time during which they would otherwise be homebound. They have enabled women to work outside the home, pursue nontraditional roles, and gain some financial independence.

Schools are presumably much more than baby-sitters, however. They teach children as well as supervise them. Often they offer the young instruction that housewives cannot provide for their own children. They teach written language and basic learning skills, and they can offer children a greater awareness of the outside world than the homebound mother may be able to stimulate.

As teachers of the young, schools have performed an especially vital function for those immigrant, illiterate, or poorly educated women whose children have populated American schools for many generations. Besides the cognitive instruction they offer the young, the schools also socialize them by teaching values and behavior and by offering opportunities for them to work and play with other children.

Such instruction of the young has benefited women to the extent that children are perceived by them as personal extensions of themselves. In this sense, the schools serve mothers by serving their children.

Modern elementary and secondary schools have played a special role in the education of female children. Despite some conspicuous problems, females are probably treated in a more egalitarian way in schools than in other institutions, including religious, familial, economic, and political institutions. In the modern school, females and males attend classes together, and in approximately the same, rather than token, numbers. They compete on an equal footing and they pursue essentially the same courses of study. The sex-segregated public school, while it thrives in some other societies, has almost vanished in the United States. Virtually nowhere in the adult working world or in adult organizations is so little sex segregation present.

Moreover, in the person of the female teacher, the female student has before her a role model on which she may pattern her own behavior and aspirations. During the formative years such role models are especially available in primary schools, where female teachers have been numerically dominant, but at no point throughout the precollege experience are they absent.

Through these role models, female students may learn that woman's "place" is not limited to the home, that women know a great deal, that they are legitimately interested in cognitive pursuits, and that they can direct the activities of others. The school principal may be a male, but his authority is far more distant than that of the classroom teacher with whom students are in constant and direct contact.

The female teacher is a special kind of role model. She is not simply a woman who works, perhaps merely to supplement family income as many women workers *say* they do. She is a highly educated and perhaps tenured career woman whose job is a serious and often a primary occupation. She is relatively well paid and she has considerable financial and intellectual autonomy. In other words, she is often a model of the "liberated woman." This model is limited, of course, in that it does not penetrate nontraditional jobs for women, but it has considerable use nonetheless as an introduction to the idea of careers for women.

In this connection, schools have benefited women in another way. In their role as employer, they have given women opportunities to pursue careers and professions in education—as teachers, counselors, nurses, administrators. In recent years about two million women have been employed as teachers below the college level. More women are so employed than are employed in all the other professions combined, except health care; and female teachers have been almost twice as numerous as female professionals in health care.

Through the years, the schools have been a primary source of steady and relatively well-paid employment for women, offering them, among other benefits, security, status in the larger society, work schedules and holidays that suit family responsibilities, and relatively stimulating and self-directed work.

The practices and ideology of school instruction also tend to reduce sexist practices in educational and other institutions. The ideology asserts that rewards should be determined by achievement, rather than by sex, race, religion, influence, or socioeconomic status. Merit and ability are stressed and ascribed status scorned as measures of distinction. If girls can compete in the same arena with boys, using the same rules, they merit the same recognition.

Most of the various school inequalities that discriminate against disadvantaged racial, ethnic, socioeconomic, or religious groups do not apply to the sexes. Such inequitable practices are usually made possible by the fact that the superior and subordinate groups live in different families, different neighborhoods, have recognizably different cultures, organized influence, and ability to pay for schooling. Such characteristics are absent or less important among males and females. That is to say, boys and girls come from the same families, the same neighborhoods and culture—and their families have the same amount of influence in the schools.

The particular measures of achievement used in schools are usually ones on which females have at least an equal chance of success in competition with boys, if not an edge in some cases. These measures are usually based on verbal responses, conduct, and motivation. Insofar as many girls may be more highly motivated to study than boys, more amenable to school codes of conduct, and more verbal than boys, they may also achieve a somewhat superior place in the school's meritocracy. So it is that the school grades of girls tend to be higher on the average than those of boys. Girls are also less likely than boys to drop out of school, and they are much less likely to become school "failures" or "misfits."

The school's ideology with respect to the larger society also serves the interests of women. This ideology, which the schools are designated to transmit to the young, stresses the ideals of freedom, civil liberties, democracy, and equality of opportunity. Such an ideology certainly legitimates the current doctrine that women are by law entitled to fair representation in occupations and places of employment. It also justifies the view, now supported by law, that female students and school staff are entitled to the same treatment, rights, and benefits as males receive.

Certain disadvantages for women may, of course, be present in the symbiotic relationship they have with primary schools. These may include the limited range of instructional resources made available to young students and the stereotypes created by the numerical predominance of female teachers in the primary years. Many female teachers have been taught rather little about the technological society to which so many male occupations relate, and so they may not be well equipped to offer such knowledge to the females (or males) they instruct.

Moreover, the predominance of females in the early childhood years, both at home and in school, may have certain negative consequences in later years as adolescents move toward adulthood and independence of parental authority. Any perceived overexposure to female authority during childhood years may lead in later years to a rejection of female authority on the job and in the larger society. Such responses may handicap women who seek policy-making and leadership roles in the working world.

2

Status, Trends, Comparatives

Although the women of the United States are confined within the narrow circle of domestic life, . . . I have nowhere seen woman occupying a loftier position; and if I were asked . . . to what the singular prosperity and growing strength of that people ought mainly to be attributed, I should reply: To the superiority of their women.

Alexis de Toqueville, Democracy in America

The educational attainment of American women compares favorably with that of males in that the median years of their schooling is almost the same. However, the distribution of their schooling is different. A significantly larger proportion of women graduate from high school, and a significantly smaller proportion complete five or more years of college.

Female high school graduates have outnumbered male graduates since at least 1869. In that year, 9,000 girls and 7,000 boys graduated from high school. In 1971-72 about 25,000 more girls than boys were high school graduates, according to HEW statistics.

A significant number of girls graduate each year from nonpublic high schools—about 156,000 in 1971-72, the largest numbers in New York (22,400), Pennsylvania (16,300), Illinois (13,200), and California (10,300).

Girls tend to stay in high school until graduation largely because they have less motive and less opportunity to find paying jobs, and the jobs that are available and desirable, especially in clerical work, usually require a high school education. At any rate, among 16- to 20-year-olds in the civilian noninstitutional population in 1971, more than a million males but only 604,000 females were high school dropouts.

Of those females who do drop out of primary or secondary schools, about two in five do so because of marriage or pregnancy. About one in four college women drop out for the same reason. Lack of interest in school is the second most common reason given by girls for dropping out, and economic need the third. Only one in eight drop out at all levels for economic reasons. This suggests that numbers of female school dropouts might be more easily reduced by making schooling both more interesting and more compatible with family life than by making it more financially accessible.

In 1970, the median years of school completed by women age 25 and over ranged from a high of 12.4 in Alaska, Colorado, Nevada, Utah, Washington, and Wyoming, to a low of 10.3 in Kentucky, 10.6 in South Carolina, 10.7 in Arkansas, and 10.8 in Georgia, Louisiana, North Carolina, Tennessee, and West Virginia. Thus, women in the West had the most median years of schooling and women in the South the fewest, according to the Bureau of the Census. Among white women, the lowest medians were found in Kentucky (10.3) and West Virginia (10.8). The median schooling of black women reached a high in states where the black population is relatively small: 12.7 years in Hawaii, 12.5 in New Hampshire, 12.3 in Alaska, Maine, and South Dakota, 12.2 in Vermont, Colorado, and Montana, and a low in states where the black population is most concentrated—Mississippi and South Carolina (8.1). The median school years for all white women age 25 and over was 12.1 in 1970. For black women it was 10.0, and for women of Spanish heritage it was 9.4.

At age 18 and 19, about 48 percent of females and only 38 percent of males are enrolled in school. From then on, female enrollment begins a sharp decline. At age 20 and 21, only 26 percent of females (and 34 percent of males) are enrolled in school. Between ages 22 and 34, the main enrollment years for advanced degrees, more than twice as many males as females are enrolled in school.

Women tend to be more homogeneous than men in their educational attainment and more highly concentrated in the middle range of attainment. Men are more dispersed over the range, more likely to be high school dropouts and more likely to be advanced degree candidates. The spread represents class and occupational differences, those in elite professional and managerial occupations being at the top and unskilled and semiskilled male workers at the bottom. In a sense, then, males are educationally both the most and the least privileged.

The overwhelming majority of women—more than 80 percent of the total—have never been to college. The largest proportion of these—about 40 percent—are high school graduates, and an additional 20 percent have had some high school but did not graduate. Less than 10 percent of all women are college graduates. In contrast, almost a quarter of women have only a grade school education or less. The seriously undereducated are, therefore, more than twice as numerous as the college educated. Certainly these figures are not reflected in the amount of attention or money devoted to the education of women.

It is important, and difficult, to keep in mind that the college woman, far from being typical, represents only a minority of women in the nation, however influential and articulate that minority may be. In most ways the educational and occupational interests of college and noncollege women are probably congruent, but noncollege women also have special needs that require special attention. Although the exploration of the needs, knowledge, and attitudes of the noncollege woman goes beyond the limits of this volume,

**Table 1. Median School Years Completed by Persons 25
Years And Over: 1960 And 1970**

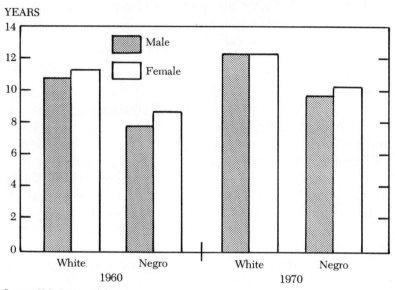

Source: U.S. Bureau of the Census

it remains a high priority for future research on women
and education.

During the sixties the proportion of women attending
college rose sharply to embrace more than a third
of female high school graduates. From 1950 to 1965
first-time college enrollments of women in credit
programs more than tripled, while high school graduation among women only doubled. By 1974 about four
million women were enrolled in degree credit programs and about 4.9 million males, representing a
six-fold increase for women and a three-fold increase
for men since 1946.

These rising enrollments undoubtedly brought a
concomitant rise in the aspirations and consciousness
of women. They certainly provided an articulate and
informed leadership for the women's movement.

On teacher ratings of achievement, girls do clearly
better than boys in primary and secondary schools.

For example, in a national longitudinal survey, 60 percent of female high school seniors and only 41 percent of males reported a grade average of B or better.

On standardized achievement tests, results are mixed. On some of these tests boys score higher than girls, mainly because of the stress on scientific knowledge in the tests. On the National Assessment of Educational Progress, girls perform better in some subjects and less well in others. In writing, for example, girls do significantly better than boys. Among 9-year-olds in 1969, the median percent of correct responses was 34.7 for females and 22.3 for males; among 17-year-olds, it was 67.0 for females and 57.3 for males. Girls also did better in reading, but boys did significantly better in science. They did about equally well in citizenship and literature.

Illiteracy

An astonishing number of American women are still illiterate: more than 727,000, about half of them under 44 years of age. The illiteracy rate of all males is only somewhat higher than that of females, but among blacks the rate for males is considerably higher than for females (4.3 percent and 2.9 percent respectively in 1970).

While American illiteracy rates are somewhat higher for males than for females, in most of the world the rates are much higher for women. About 28 percent of all adult males and almost 40 percent of all adult women in the world's population are illiterate.

Female illiteracy is higher on all the continents. In Africa, 84 percent of adult women and 63 percent of adult males are illiterate. In the Arab states, 86 percent of women and 61 percent of males are illiterate, in Asia 57 percent of women and 37 percent of males, in Latin America 27 percent of women and 20 percent of males, in Europe 5 percent of women and about

Table 2.   Percentage of Population Illiterate in Specific
Countries
(Illiteracy: inability to read and write)

Country	Age	Male	Female
Algeria	15–24	35.4	69.7
	65 plus	84.1	99.6
Libyan Arab Republic	15–19	31.3	84.6
	65 plus	88.9	99.6
Morocco	15–19	44.9	73.6
	65 plus	81.4	97.5
South Africa (Bantu)	15–24	51.0	46.0
Zambia	15–19	14.9	29.1
Mexico	15–19	13.9	16.1
	40 plus	31.2	43.3
U.S.	16–24	.3	.2
	65 plus	3.4	3.5
Brazil	15–19	25.8	23.0
	65 plus	46.0	61.2
Venezuela	15–19	25.5	25.0
	65 plus	57.0	58.9
Indonesia	15–19	26.7	44.5
	65 plus	83.6	96.2
Philippines	15–19	15.9	13.6
	65 plus	60.8	76.8
Turkey	15–19	13.9	39.1
	65 plus	74.0	92.7

Source: UNESCO "Statistical Yearbook," 1972.

22.5 percent of males, and in North America about
2 percent of women and 1 percent of men.

These comparative figures indicate that female illiteracy in the world's population is still high but that
considerable progress in reducing these rates has been
made in virtually all parts of the world during recent
decades. In most countries, the majority of people
over age 65 and a much lower percentage of the younger
population are illiterate.

In most of the world's population a fairly even
balance is being achieved in enrollments of males

and females in all three educational levels, primary, secondary, and higher schools. In North and South America, women are 48 percent of all enrollments, in the USSR 49 percent, in Europe 47 percent, in Africa 39 percent, in Asia (excluding Arab states) 38 percent, and in the Arab states 35 percent.

In higher education, however, the enrollments of women still lag behind those of males, though considerable progress has been made even at this level. Among world school enrollments, women are 43 percent of the total. At the first level, they are 44 percent of the total, at the second 43 percent, and at the third (college equivalent) 38 percent.

Teaching

Earlier in the century, teaching was much more a female profession than it is now. The phenomenal growth of secondary and especially higher education greatly diminished the numerical dominance of women. In 1970, male teachers, including those in higher education, almost equalled the number of female teachers—1.2 million and 1.7 million respectively. In 1930, women teachers were almost four times as numerous as males—819,000 and 216,000 respectively.

Table 3.   Percentage of Women Among All Teachers in Selected Years

	Elementary	Secondary	Elementary and Secondary
1957–58	87.2	49.6	73.2
1960–61	85.8	47.2	70.7
1963–64	85.5	46.1	68.9
1966–67	85.4	64.0	68.3
1970–71	84.7	45.9	67.2
1971–72	84.5	45.8	66.9

Source: *Estimates of School Statistics, 1971-72,* National Education Association, Research Report, 1971-73.

Table 4. Estimated Number and Percent Distribution of Full-Time Public School Professional Employees, 1970-71, by Sex
(Instructional Staff and Central Office)

Position	Number of Persons			Percent Distribution		
1	Total 2	Men 3	Women 4	Total 5	Men 6	Women 7
Instructional Staff:						
Teachers	2,034,581	667,751	1,366,830	100.0%	32.8%	67.2%
Principals:						
Elementary	40,453	32,605	7,848	100.0	80.6	19.4
Elementary-teaching principals	7,261	5,068	2,193	100.0	69.8	30.2
Junior-high	8,782	8,472	310	100.0	96.5	3.5
Senior-high	13,763	13,349	414	100.0	97.0	3.0
Total principals	70,259	59,494	10,765	100.0	84.7	15.3
Assistant principals:						
Elementary	5,119	3,388	1,731	100.0	66.2	33.8
Junior-high	6,777	6,022	755	100.0	88.9	11.1
Senior-high	11,403	10,383	1,020	100.0	91.1	8.9
Total assistant principals	23,299	19,793	3,506	100.0	85.0	15.0
Other instructional staff:						
Heads of departments	12,478	8,639	3,839	100.0	69.2	30.8
School librarians	30,757	2,658	28,099	100.0	8.6	91.4
Counselors	39,348	20,897	18,451	100.0	53.1	46.9
Social workers and/or visiting teachers	6,002	1,051	4,951	100.0	17.5	82.5
Psychologists and psychometrists	3,980	1,827	2,153	100.0	45.9	54.1

	Number			Percent		
School nurses	15,639	126	15,513	100.0	0.8	99.2
Other or not stated	563	235	328	100.0	41.7	58.3
Total other instructional staff	108,767	35,433	73,334	100.0	32.6	67.4
Total instructional staff	2,236,906	782,471	1,454,435	100.0	35.0	65.0
Central Office Administrators:						
Superintendents	14,379	14,289	90	100.0	99.4	0.6
Deputy and associate superintendents	731	676	55	100.0	92.5	7.5
Assistant superintendents	4,402	4,276	126	100.0	97.1	2.9
Administrative assistants to the superintendent	2,345	1,989	356	100.0	84.8	15.2
Administrators for:						
General administration[a]	10,414	5,398	5,016	100.0	51.8	48.2
Finance and school plant[b]	6,980	6,390	590	100.0	91.5	8.5
Pupil personnel services[c]	7,510	4,636	2,874	100.0	61.7	38.3
Instructional administration[d]	10,881	5,846	5,035	100.0	53.7	46.3
Special subject areas[e]	7,664	4,891	2,773	100.0	63.8	36.2
Total central-office administrators	65,306	48,391	16,915	100.0	74.1	25.9
Total full-time professional employees	2,302,212	830,862	1,471,350	100.0%	36.1%	63.9%

[a]Comprises staff personnel, research, food services, health services, pupil transportation, community relations, publications, and/or information, and federal and/or state grants and aids.

[b]Comprises general finance, purchasing, accounting and auditing, data processing, buildings—operation and maintenance, and buildings—planning and construction.

[c]Comprises general personnel, attendance, guidance, and testing psychological and psychiatric services, and programs for the disadvantaged.

[d]Comprises general, elementary education, secondary education, adult education, special education, library services, instructional materials, and audiovisual education.

[e]Comprises art, home economics, industrial arts, music, physical and health education, vocational education, mathematics and/or science, English and/or reading, foreign languages, social sciences, and other.

Source: National Education Association, Research Division, Research Report 1971-R5.

Males are also a much larger proportion of elementary and secondary school teachers than they were in 1930. In 1970, women were twice as numerous as men at these levels, but in 1930 they had been about five times as numerous. The change resulted from the growth of secondary schools and the shift to the employment of males at this level. In 1930 women had been twice as numerous as males among secondary school teachers; now they are somewhat less numerous.

Even in higher education, the proportion of women faculty has decreased. In 1930, males were somewhat more than twice as numerous as women in college faculties. Now they are about three times as numerous.

The proportion of male teachers who have degrees beyond the bachelor's is more than twice as great as the proportion of females with them, according to the NEA. About 43 percent of male public school teachers had a master's degree or its equivalent in 1970, but only 19 percent of female teachers. Since rank and compensation in the educational hierarchy are influenced by degrees held, this difference may at least partly explain the subordinate status of women in the teaching profession.

While the median years of teaching experience was the same in 1970 for male and female public school teachers, the average annual salary of male teachers was $9,900 and that of female teachers only $9,000.

Among secondary school teachers, women are highly concentrated in English departments. Almost a third of all women secondary school teachers (29 percent) taught English in 1970, compared with only 13 percent of men. Other areas of study that employed large numbers of women were: math (13 percent compared with 15 percent of males); home economics (11 percent of women and no males); health and physical education (10 percent of women and 7 percent of males). Women were extremely under-represented in science (3 percent of women and 17 percent of males); in industrial arts and vocational education (.5 percent of women, all

of them in "vocational" education, and 11 percent
of males); and in social studies (7 percent of women
and 20 percent of men).

Though the status of women in the total teaching
profession is a subordinate one, so far as authority,
income, and subjects taught are concerned, it is nonetheless true that women are a numerical majority in
the profession and that their position in the profession
is probably stronger than the position of women
elsewhere in the world.

Nowhere in the western world has there been as
high a proportion of women primary school teachers
as in the United States. In Great Britain and Sweden,
the closest rivals, women have been 75 percent of
primary school teachers, in France 66 percent, and
in Finland 63 percent. Among both secondary and
postsecondary teachers, women have been a higher
proportion of the total in the United States than in
any country except France. In postsecondary schools,
women are 20 percent of teachers in the United States,
21 percent in France, 18 percent in Finland, 13 percent
in Canada, 11 percent in Great Britain, 10 percent
in Sweden, 8 percent in Austria, 2 percent in West
Germany.

To state these facts is not to offer praise for the
status of women in the American teaching profession;
it is only to suggest that women elsewhere have even
further to go.

Historical Backgrounds

3

Women in Classical and Medieval Education

Historically, the education of women has been fashioned around the tasks and roles they perform in the society, just as male education has been. The roles of women, almost to the present day, have been limited chiefly to domestic ones—the bearing and rearing of children, cooking, making clothing, and keeping house. It has been assumed that these domestic tasks are so simple to perform, and so easy to pass on from one generation to the next, that they require no special preparation, knowledge, or schooling. Given these roles and these views of the limited complexity—and social contribution—of the roles, it is little wonder that the education of women, almost until the modern period, has been so universally neglected.

Women of rank and leisure have, in some societies at least, developed interests and knowledge extending beyond the strictly domestic duties. For these women, social roles have usually also extended beyond their households. In some places, women of lesser rank have acquired vocational skills—as well as religious learning and vocations—that reach beyond the strictly domestic. Women's work and education have generally been confined, however, to household duties.

The history of the education of women has been as neglected as their education. The modern treatment of the subject is sketchy at best; no comprehensive

volume on any given historic period exists, and virtually nothing at all gives an overview of the history
of women in education. The records are there, buried
in the main body of history and literature, and some
rather devoted digging may be required to extricate
them. What is known may be intriguing enough to
stimulate such excavations.

The ancient Greeks are a special case in history.
Roman, Byzantine, medieval, and modern learning all
have deep roots in classical Greek learning, culture,
arts, literature, philosophy, and politics. Moreover, the
New Testament of the Christian Bible was written
first in Greek, and the gospels were spread by Greek-
speaking apostles. Ancient Greek democracy, much
admired in the modern world, was, as we know, based
on slavery. Perhaps less well known is the fact that
Greek women occupied a status not much more exalted
than that of slaves.

The ancient Greek city has been called a "men's
club," a warrior and seafaring community that excluded women from its inner circles. The Greek style of
education tended to be a male-to-male tutorial, often
involving a close personal, even sexual, relationship
between an older and a younger male. The family
was not a strong institution. It carried on only limited
education of the young, and mothers were generally
considered unfit to teach their own children, while
fathers were busy with the duties of citizenship. At
about age seven, young boys began their education
under the tutorship of older males. Girls stayed at
home with mother.

In the early Greek period, there were no schools.
Later, when they did appear, they were often disdained
by the Greek citizen because they charged fees and
taught mainly technical subjects.

A few women's schools existed. Sappho of Lesbos,
most notably, operated a school that taught women
of rank such subjects as singing, music, dancing, and

sports. Considerable variation in the status of women can, of course, be found among the Greek cities. Among Spartans, for example, women were regarded mainly as breeders of sons and warriors, for which task they were expected to train their bodies and keep themselves physically fit. In Greece as elsewhere (in Hitler's Germany, for example), the stronger the military ethic and the more segregated the male military class, the more degraded the status of women tended to be.

The Romans adopted much of Greek learning and culture. They rejected, however, two central features: music, which the Greeks had regarded as their highest art form, and sport, which the Romans regarded as useless and—in its nudity and associations with homosexuality in Greece—shocking. Unfortunately, both sport and music were activities in which Greek women had actively participated; such participation was generally denied Roman women.

The Romans apparently had quite a different view from the Greeks of the family and its functions. The Roman family was a strong institution, and the Romans regarded the family circle as the proper place for the child to grow up and receive an education. The mother raised and taught her own children, rather than pass on the duty to slaves or male tutors. Even the most aristocratic Roman women were said to feel honored to assume a place in the family as the guardian and teacher of the young.

As in Greece, however, the male child at age seven ceased to be under the exclusive guardianship of his mother. His new tutor was his father—rather than an adult male outside the family, as was the case in Greece. The father was thought to be the male child's real teacher, and when other males performed this function, they were expected to act like fathers. Girls, again, stayed at home with mother. At about age 16, the education of the aristocratic Roman boy moved outside the family, first with preparation for public

life, and then with military service. The education
of women seldom went beyond the confines of the
household.

The Dark Ages, by their very name, are taken to
be a time of ignorance, ominous gloom, and suppres-
sion of learning and inquiry. So far as women are
concerned, the spread of Christianity throughout the
Roman Empire led in the direction of greater participation in family and religious life. In the medieval
Christian world, women took on, in effect, a most
significant and new social role. They became important
guardians and propagators of the faith, in their own
lives, in the instruction of their children, in the
teaching they received in convents, as nuns of religious
orders, and as servants of the church in a variety of
roles.

It is estimated, indeed, that more women than men
were literate during the Middle Ages—and on into
the Renaissance. The Catholic stress on family life
and on monogamy gave women a secure and significant
place in their homes and in society. Women were
expected to bring up children in their religious faith
and maintain a Christian household. They played a
leading role in religious life. Mary, mother of Jesus,
was an exalted figure in the faith (more so, perhaps,
than any comparable figure in other faiths), and women
served the church as benefactors, staff, and servants.

Women were (and are), however, denied admission
to the priesthood and the high offices of the church,
and, moreover, priests were pledged to celibacy. Thus,
sex roles in the church were both sharply segregated
and hierarchical, and the education of the sexes tended
to reflect these differences. In medieval Europe, the
main purpose of the university was to train males
for the priesthood. It was in these institutions that
most of the scholarship of the period was promoted
and from them most publications were issued.

Women entered convents to train for the nunnery
and religious vocations and, if they were women of

rank, to train for their domestic and religious functions.
Some churchmen of the time even thought that women,
by training in medicine, theology, and service, could
be sent as missionaries to conquer the infidel, as the
crusaders had been unable to do.

In the fourteenth century, Geoffrey de la Tour-
Landry's book on chivalry, a popular text of its day,
advised brides on how to win prestige and wealth
through honor and obedience. He was apparently the
Dale Carnegie of his day. The popularity of this book
certainly indicated that many women of the time were
able to read. In the lower schools of France in that
century, girls were educated alongside boys, and in
Germany, there were more cloisters for females than
for males.

In fifteenth-century Italy, women played an important part in the revival of humanist learning and of
the Roman and Greek classics. They also won honors
in the sciences and arts, and the universities, opened
to women in the late medieval period, began to award
them the doctorate. Women lectured at the universities
on religion, philosophy, and literature. During the
Renaissance the intellectual development of women
went even further. Women of the upper class and
even business and professional women became so
versed in the classics that visitors to Italy marvelled
at their learning and began to encourage classical
studies for their own women. Such studies often
included poetry, oratory, Roman history, the ethics
of Roman Stoicism, Greek, mathematics, geometry,
astronomy, music, singing.

Burckhardt observes:

> In order to understand the higher forms of social intercourse
> during the Renaissance, it is necessary to know that woman
> was regarded as in a position of perfect equality with man.
> Above all, the education of the woman among the higher
> classes is essentially the same as that of the man. There
> was not the slightest hesitation among the Italians of the
> Renaissance in according the same literary and even philo-

logical instruction to sons and daughters. There was no
question of a conscious "emancipation" of woman or any-
thing so out of the ordinary, for the situation was understood
to be a matter of course. The education of the woman of
rank, just as well as that of the man, sought the development
of a well-rounded personality in every respect.

Even Boccaccio in fourteenth-century Italy wrote
his *De Claris Mulieribus* about outstanding women,
including Eve, Cleopatra, Sappho, and the Queen of
Naples. In the fifteenth century, the German writer
Agrippa wrote a similar volume on the excellence,
even superiority, of women. Queen Isabella of Spain
became so enamored of the new learning that she
hired Italian instructors to teach in her court and
in the universities. She studied the classics herself
and personally supervised the instruction of others.

Women of the Middle Ages and Renaissance were
also especially supportive of the mystical tendencies
of the time and of the religious teachings that began
with experience and intuition, rather than rationality
and book-learning, and of the mystical orders that
mixed with people of all ranks and abjured riches
and privilege.

Women were also active participants in the medieval
guilds, where they received training from which our
own apprenticeship programs are direct descendants.
It is firmly established that women were admitted
to the guilds, usually as the widows of guild members
who had died. *English Guilds,* a volume edited by J.
T. Smith, presents original documents, mainly from
the fourteenth century, giving essential facts about
the English guilds. These documents were available
because Parliament in 1389 had required that local
governments and guilds submit records of "bretheren
and sisteren" in all English shires.

Most of the guilds cited in these medieval documents
were social and religious organizations, but there were
also many crafts guilds among them. Of the eighty-five
craft guilds on which Smith offered records, at least

seventy-two had women members admitted on an equal basis with men. In many cases, women were admitted as widows because they had worked beside their husbands in their shop, doing the same work, and carrying on the same supervision of apprentices. Nine guilds appear to have been entirely male: The Guild of Young Scholars at Lynn (perhaps preparing for the priesthood); the guilds of shipmen at Lynn; smiths at Chesterfield; fullers at Bristol; tailors, cordwainers, and bakers at Exeter. Women had equal membership in the guilds of: barbers, furriers, carpenters, saddlers, and spurriers at Norwich; fullers, tailors, and tylers at Lincoln; joiners and carpenters at Worcester. Women also belonged to the religious and benevolent guilds.

In all these guilds, the rights and responsibilities of women were apparently the same as for men. They helped elect officers and they took part in all proceedings. That women were far from passive members is evidenced by the guild rules that often forbade disorderly debates by both the "sisteren" and the "bretheren."

On the continent, women were also members of many guilds and had a few of their own. In Italy, the guilds prospered essentially in places most remote from Rome and central authority, and women were usually included in the most prosperous.

Georges Francois Renard in his *Guilds in the Middle Ages*, concludes:

> It would be a mistake to imagine that the woman of the Middle Ages was confined to her home and was ignorant of the difficulties of a worker's life. In those days she had an economic independence, such as is hardly to be met with in our own time. In many countries she possessed, for instance, the power to dispose of her property without her husband's permission. It is therefore natural that there should be women's guilds organized and administered like those of men. They existed in exclusively feminine crafts: fifteen of them were to be found in Paris alone towards

the end of the thirteenth century, in the dressmaking industry
and among the silk-workers and goldthread workers especially.

Matilda, Countess of Tuscany, born 1046, was the
sole heir of Italy's richest estate, and she took considerable interest in the guilds of Florence, her leading
city, protecting them and encouraging them. Matilda,
educated by her mother, Beatrice of Bar, spoke Italian,
French, and German and wrote in Latin.

When Venice rose from the sea to become the Queen
of the Adriatic, it was through the aid of numerous
skilled women workers, many of them guild members,
who built the bridges and constructed the buildings
for this great Italian city.

In thirteenth-century Paris, about eighty mixed
guilds admitted widows to carry on their husband's
workshops. Men sometimes tried to exclude women
from the guilds. The bakers of Pontoise, for example,
seeking a monopoly on bread baking, claimed that
women were not strong enough to knead bread and
so should be excluded. The French Parliament thought
otherwise.

During the medieval period, the Roman Catholic
Church generally claimed an exclusive right to operate
schools, most of them having a uniform curriculum
that included few scientific or technological studies.
The establishment of convents for the education of
women opened new avenues of learning to them, for
if women were to perform their religious functions,
they needed to receive religious instruction. The benefits were real, but, excluded from the priesthood and
assigned by ancient beliefs and traditions to separate
and usually subservient roles, the extent of their
education was inevitably limited.

The Reformation introduced some educational variety and a break with many of the religious traditions
that placed strictures on the education of women.
Protestants emphasized the need for individuals to

read and interpret the testaments on their own, dispensing with the priestly intermediary. Secular and public schools arose, opening many nontraditional opportunities to women. But it was chiefly industrialization that assigned new social roles to women and made it possible for them to engage in studies that ranged well beyond their traditional family and religious functions.

Certainly religious faith and belief have powerful influences on the mind and on the direction that education will take. In societies where paternalistic and traditional religions dominate education—as in societies where the military or other male institutions are dominant—women have usually suffered most from educational discrimination and segregation.

4

Strictures on Women: French and British

The respective employments of the male and female sex being different, a different mode of education is consequently required. For whatever quality there may be in the natural powers of their minds . . . yet the female sex, from their situation in life, and from the duties corresponding with it, must evidently be instructed in a manner suitable to the tasks which they will have to perform.

To be obedient daughters, faithful wives; and prudent mothers; to be useful in the affairs of the house; to be sensible companions, and affectionate friends, are, without doubt, the principal objects of female duty.

—*F. Burton,* Lectures on Female Education and Manners, *1793.*

I n the seventeenth and eighteenth centuries, writing and preaching about the duties and training of women became, among religious men, a rather popular undertaking. At any rate, a number of these lectures and "strictures" have been retrieved from history and are now available, including the following two. They are quoted from at some length here because they transmit some firsthand sense of what life and education were like for women several centuries ago. Both views—one Catholic, one Protestant—were regarded as enlightened for their time because they were concerned about the need to educate women.

Fénelon, born in 1651 into an aristocratic French

family, became a Catholic priest and a prominent
educator in his day.

Nothing is more neglected than the education of girls.
Custom and the caprice of mothers often decide the whole
matter. The education of boys is regarded as a most important
matter because of its bearing on the public weal. Reference
is invariably made to the numerous women whose intellectual attainments have made them ridiculous.

A woman's intellect is normally more feeble and her
curiosity greater than those of a man; also it is undesirable
to set her to studies which may turn her head. Women
should not govern the state or make war or enter the sacred
ministry. Thus they can dispense with some of the more
difficult branches of knowledge. Even the majority of the
mechanical arts are not suitable to them. They are made
for exercise in moderation. Their bodies as well as their
minds are less strong and robust than those of men. On
the other hand, nature has given them as a recompense
industry, neatness, and economy, so as to keep them quietly
occupied in their homes.

But what results from this natural weakness of women?
The weaker they are the more important it is to strengthen
them. The world is not an abstraction; it is the sum total
of families; and who can civilize it more effectively than
women?

They (the duties of women) are scarcely less important
to the public than those of men, since women have a
household to rule, a husband to make happy, and children
to bring up well. They form half of the human race redeemed
by the blood of Jesus Christ and destined to eternal life.

Ignorance is the reason for a girl being bored and not
knowing how to occupy herself. Having nothing to do the
girl abandons herself to idleness; and idleness is a weakness
of the soul, and inexhaustible source of boredom. When
this softness and indolence are joined to ignorance there
results a dangerous inclination towards amusements and
entertainments. This indeed it is which excites an indiscreet
and insatiable curiosity. Those who are well-educated and
occupied in serious pursuits have as a rule only a moderate
curiosity.

Those who have intelligence often develop into bluestockings and read every book which can feed their vanity. They develop a passion for novels, for plays, for fanciful tales of adventure with a romantic love interest. These adventures which the fiction-writer invents in order to please, have no relation to the motives which hold sway in real life and which decide actual events, nor to the disappointments which one meets in whatever one takes in hand. She longs to live like these imaginary princesses who in novels are always charming, always worshipped, always independent. How she will hate to descend from this romance to the sordid details of housekeeping!

Some girls push their curiosity still further and take upon themselves to express opinions on religious matters, although they are incapable of doing so. But those who have insufficient intellectual aptitude for these curiosities, still have others proportionate to their powers. They want to be told everything and to tell everything. They are vain and vanity makes them talkative. They are frivolous and their frivolity prevents the reflection which would often help them to keep silence.

We must also repress in them inordinate friendships, trivial jealousies, exaggerated compliments, and transports. All this spoils them and accustoms them to regard as too humdrum and stiff whatever is grave and serious. We should even try to induce them to study how to speak in a short and concise manner. True intelligence is shown in cutting out any useless discourse and saying much in a few words; instead of which most women say little in many words. They take readiness of speech and vivacity of imagination for intelligence.

Nothing good can be expected from a woman unless she can be induced to consider and examine her thoughts, to explain them in a concise manner, and to know when to be silent. Another thing which contributes very much to the long-winded discourses of women is that they are by nature artificial and use long detours before they come to the point. They have a high opinion of craftiness—and why should they not, since they know nothing of a better kind of prudence. They have a pliable nature which enables them to play easily all sorts of parts. Tears cost them nothing; their passions are quick and their knowledge limited.

We may add that they are diffident and full of false

modesty; and this again is a cause of pretence. The means
to prevent so great a fault is never to give them an opportunity
for being crafty, but to accustom them to say frankly what
they feel about any permissible subject. They should be
free to express their boredom when they feel bored. They
should never be forced to appear as if they liked certain
persons or books if they do not like them.

Above all never let girls suspect that you want them
to aspire to become nuns, for this thought destroys their
confidence in their parents, suggests to them that they are
not loved.

The chief fault to be found in girls is vanity. They are
born with an eager desire to please. As the avenues which
lead men to positions of authority and to glory are closed
to them they try to compensate for this by graces of the
mind or of the body. This explains their sweet and insinuat-
ing way of talking and why they aim so much at being
beautiful, and at possessing a charming appearance. This
excess is more marked among our nation than in any other.
The instability of disposition which is common among us
causes a continual change in the fashions, so that to the
love of dress is added that of novelty which has a curious
attraction for the female mind.

Beauty, you will say, deceives the person who possesses
it more than those who are dazzled by it. Persons who
seek all their distinction from their good looks soon become
ridiculous. Without noticing it they arrive at a certain age
when their beauty fades and when they are still charmed
with themselves, although the world, far from being so,
is disgusted with them.

As a rule the fashions are a matter of caprice. Those
who are most shallow-minded and least educated draw the
rest after them. It is enough that something has been
fashionable for a long time for it to be so no longer, and
for something else, however ridiculous, to take its place
and be admired so long as it is considered a novelty.

Jesus Christ teaches us to place all our virtue in the
fear and distrust of self. Would you wish, you could say
to a girl, to endanger your own soul and that of your neighbor
for the sake of a foolish vanity? Be horrified therefore at
these bare necks and other immodesties. Above all never
allow girls to dress above their rank. Show them the danger

to which they are exposing themselves and how they make themselves despised by sensible people if they forget their position.

A more puritanical tone is struck by the Protestant minister, the Rev. John Bennett, in his *Strictures on Female Education* (Source Book Press, published in 1795.)

When we consider the natural equality of women with the other sex, their influence upon society, and their original destination to be companions and comforters of man; when we recollect the pleasures derived from their agreeable vivacity and sprightliness, the soothing tenderness of their friendship and the ardency of their affection, when we call to mind all their charms and attractions, above all, when we reflect, that the youth of both sexes are under their management for many of those early years, when all the durable impressions must be made, it may justly appear a matter of amazement, that their education has been so much and so generally neglected; that no nation, ancient or modern, has esteemed it an object of public importance, that no philosopher or legislator has interwoven it with his system, nor any writer deemed it a subject worth of a full or serious discussion.

Many famous authors of Greece and Rome, of modern Europe, and of our own country, have formed an ignominious phalanx, to wage, in inky armor, an unequal battle against this tender and defenseless sex. Even the sacred books of Revelation have been called in to sanction these malevolent effusions, and, because Solomon declaimed, at an early period, only against the worst and most abandoned of the sex, he has been followed by a number of servile imitators.

Among the Egyptians, who were celebrated for their learning, astronomy, and Magi, women met with some partial and some distinguishing marks of attention. They were admitted to the public lectures in philosophy; the laurel of science was not supposed improper for their brow; and, by a taste, unparalleled and unheard of in any other country, they were entrusted with the management of negotiations, of commercial interests and other public undertakings. But this was erring in another ridiculous extreme. It was at-

tempting to make them move in a sphere, for which nature
never gave them talents, nor providence designed them.
The sort of knowledge, which these sages communicated,
unmade the women. It raised her understanding on the
ruin of her graces.

[The Babylonian and Assyrian] shocking and indelicate
custom of collecting all their young, marriageable women,
and disposing of their charms and persons by auction, whilst
it brings a blush on every modest cheek, may abundantly
convince us, that this people had but slender ideas of female
importance, of any *moral* qualities in the sex, or any *mental*
perfections. The Medes and Persians afford us no specimens
of any great partiality exercised to the fair.

It is certain the Greeks were the very patterns of every
thing that could be charming and exquisite in taste. The
truth is, eloquence and valour were the sole, exclusive
ambition of the times. As yet, women had not emerged
from a low and inglorious condition of servility. As taste,
however, gradually advanced, and knowledge made the
feelings exquisitely alive, the Greeks began ardently to pant
for an intercourse with the sex: And, to the eternal disgrace
of their morality, they found it in their *courtezans*. In reality,
it was not so much a matter of wickedness, as of taste.
While women of modesty were deprived of all advantages
for improving themselves, these courtezans, by mixing in
public circles, had acquired all the interesting allurements
and attractions. Hence the unbounded attentions they received. Hence the most learned men had interviews at their
houses. Amongst such a people what was female education?
While modesty was thus openly violated and shocked, where
was moral discipline, culture, and improvement?

Though in the ages of chivalry, women received a kind
of adoration, and numbered in their service, such a pompous
crowd of heroes, warriors, and knights, yet this appears
not to have proceeded from that heart-felt esteem.

A woman, issuing out laws, disputing in philosophy,
haranguing the Pope in Latin, writing in Greek, studying
Hebrew, commencing theologian, and preaching in public,
may be a literary *heroine*, that challenges our wonder, but
has nothing of that softness, timidity, and reserve, which,
in that sex, so powerfully captivate our hearts, and enchant
our imaginations. To this spirit of chivalry, however, women
owe an *eternal* obligation. It was this which called them

forth from confinement and obscurity into public attention.

Whilst the institution of chivalry rendered women of such unusual consequence, and celebrated all their charms with eulogies in *Europe,* a lawgiver and a religion had sprung up in Asia, which rigidly doomed them to an inglorious confinement, as mere objects of the sensual and fugitive delight. In Africa, or the wilds of America, it is vain to expect a better fate, or a more respectful attention to females. Savages of *all* countries, indolent and cruel, take advantage of superior strength to oppress the weaker sex.

In Britain, when women are of age to discriminate, and lay in a stock of ideas, we send them to a boarding school to learn, what? Music, dancing, accomplishments, dissipation, and intrigue—everything but solid knowledge—everything but humility—everything but piety.

Though the French ladies, by being educated in convents, and there relieving the uniformity and loneliness of their prison with entertaining books, and afterwards by a constant intercourse with the other sex, have acquired considerable knowledge and refinement, yet . . . it is obvious to any discerning observer, that female literature, in this country, is swelled beyond its *natural* dimensions. France, indeed, is so far from being any proper model of female education, that I conceive it to be the vitiated taste of this people, which, set off with a graceful and bewitching manner, has infected many other countries of Europe, but particularly, their own, and overwhelmed them, at least, with a deluge of frivolity, if not of crimes.

The depraved education of females in Italy, is abundantly obvious from every page of their writers. We trace it sufficiently in . . . a custom, which degrades a husband into the mere, passive, uncomplaining beholder of nameless indiscretions. (It may be necessary, perhaps, to inform some readers, that, when an Italian Lady is married, she chooses for herself a Cecisbeo or Gallant, who is to be her almost inseparable attendant, to pay her all the petit attentions, do for her a thousand kind offices, escourt her to public places, and frequently take airings with her in her carriage.)

In Spain, whether the true spirit of philosophy has never yet been able to penetrate, and where the bigotry of a dark and clogging religion still reigns in all its force, we are delighted with the sight of many beautiful women, but have no pleasure from contemplating their character or education. On the minds of this people, the ancient rage of Knight Errantry has, still, left such a wild and romantic enthusiasm, that a woman, happening to be left alone with a man, would consider herself as highly neglected, if a sensibility to her charms did not prompt him to such *indecent* liberties with her person, as the females of most other countries would esteem an indignity, and think themselves obliged to punish with *eternal* resentment. With such sentiments, how fallen and how undesirable is woman!

Like other great warriors, the King of Prussia (Frederick) has been swallowed up with views, of too immense a nature, to attend, in any great degree, to the softness, to the charms and blandishments of woman. He has studied more the fecundity of their nature, than the formation of their minds. If monasteries are no longer to immure in chains and darkness, the weeping or misguided fair, it is not that they may become intelligent companions, or diffuse a softer charm and lustre on society; but only that they may turn out more prolific mothers, and more robust and healthy nurses of embryo heroes, warriors . . . to carry on his vast schemes. Still their milky bosoms are supposed to comprise all their virtues and their charms.

Over the immense territory of Russia, a darkness and a barbarism have, hitherto, prevailed, which obstruct every idea of female, or indeed any other species of cultivation. And though the present adventuring spirit of the Empress (Catherine) wishes to make Petersburgh the residence of the arts, civilization, and politeness, yet there is little in her character to encourage the hope of any great attention to the women of her kingdom.

Boarding schools trample upon nature, and give us artificial creatures, artificial looks, and artificial smiles. The *fine ladies* they send into the world, feel themselves ridiculously exalted above (what they conceive to be) the *groveling* offices of family economy, or domestick attentions.

Almost every thing in and about these seminaries, has a tendency to corrupt the heart. What is it these fair pupils are taught to pant for? Admiration. What are considered as the steps to it? Elegant dress, appearance, equipage, wit, smartness, dancing, singing. In the meantime what becomes of the *love of God*, which Christianity represents, as the first of duties?

5

The American Experience

The Coeducational High School, 1923

One hears conversation constantly about the young of the species, their misdeeds in deportment, their freedom from conventions, their scanty clothing upon occasion, (female); their hip-pocket flask (male); the coeducational cigarette, long motor rides following dances, presumably for cooling-off purposes, 'petting,' whatever that means. Much is said about their lack of restraint in their discussions in mixed groups; they are reputed very frank concerning sex—whatever that means. Most of these things are said by folk at least a generation older than the youth criticized and folk whose sympathies are a bit withered. . . .

The critics we need to concern ourselves with the most are the women who can only half think but who are earnestly trying to improve the world. Some of these are in Women's Clubs. . . . They are doing the damage because they talk too much. If they can be induced whenever met just to stop discussing the subject, I believe it will die out very quickly.

Elsie Davies, Glenville High School, Cleveland, "False Reports about High Schools," in Report of the Tenth Annual Meeting of National Association of Deans of Women, Dept. of Superintendents, NEA, Feb. 26, 1923, p. 148.

The education of women in colonial America was modeled on the English system. Women were trained at home for domestic work or they entered apprenticeships with a master and his family. As in England, the master of the household was responsible for the education of everyone in the household, including relatives and apprentices.

Virginia and Massachusetts laws adopted in 1642 made the head of household legally responsible for the education of all those in the household. A Virginia law of 1672 made it possible for the courts to take children from parents who could not bring them up and place them in apprenticeship with masters who were then responsible for their education. Massachusetts required family heads to teach not only reading but also the laws of the colony and the codes of Puritanism.

Discipline was more difficult in the colonial family than in the traditional English household, so by the early eighteenth century, schools for apprentices became common in the colonies. Fathers, as family heads, were thus relieved of much of the responsibility for educating and offering job training to the young.

Women also came increasingly to take on these family education roles, although most of them were poorly equipped for the job. Fewer than 40 percent of women who signed legal documents in New England in the first half of the eighteenth century could write their own names. Sixty percent made only a mark. In the whole population, those who could write were probably much fewer in numbers, because only the more literate people had much occasion to sign legal documents.

On the eve of the Revolution, the daily tasks of women tended to require only sufficient literacy to allow them to read the Bible or religious sermons. In 1775, Abigail Foote of Connecticut wrote in her diary of daily tasks:

Fix'd gown for Prude
Mend Mother's Riding-hood
Spun short thread
Fix'd tow gowns for Welsh's girls
Carded tow
Spun linen
Worked on Cheese-basket
Hatchel'd flax with Hannah, we did 51 lbs. a-piece

Pleated and ironed
Read a sermon of Doddridge's
Spooled a piece
Milked the cows
Spun linen, did 50 knots
Made a Broom of Guinea-wheat straw
Spun thread to whiten
Set a Red dye
Had two scholars from Mrs. Taylor's
I carded two pounds of whole wool and felt Nationaly
Spun harness twine, scoured the pewter.

(*E. C. B. Buel*, The Tale of the Spinning Wheel, p. 56)

By the end of the eighteenth century, the view was current both in the colonies and in Europe that women performed a significant social role and that they needed schooling of a useful variety so that they could perform their duties better.

Earlier in the eighteenth century, some Dame Schools had been set up in the homes of local women to offer girls a year or two of basic instruction, usually limited to the Three Rs. Beyond that, girls were taught such subjects as dancing, painting, drawing, writing, and French—rather impractical studies for provincial, frontier women.

It was not until 1769, on the eve of the Revolution, that girls were admitted to Boston's public schools. After the Revolution, town schools throughout New England were generally opened to girls.

The effort to build a new nation free of colonial rule turned increasingly to the education of women. Coeducational primary schools had become common, and in 1824 the first public high school "for girls only" was opened in Worcester, Massachusetts. Separate schools for girls were expensive, however. The first coeducational public high school was opened in 1826 in Bridgewater, Connecticut, and shortly thereafter high schools became generally coeducational. By mid-nineteenth century, the coeducational high school was firmly established. On his return to France in

1833, Alexis de Tocqueville, writing about the education of American women, commented:

> No free communities ever existed without morals, and
> . . . morals are the work of woman. Among almost all
> Protestant nations young women are far more the mistresses
> of their own actions than they are in Catholic countries.
> In the United States the doctrines of Protestantism are
> combined with great political liberty and a most democratic
> state of society, and nowhere are young women surrendered
> so early or so completely to their own guidance.
>
> I have been frequently surprised and almost frightened
> at the singular address and happy boldness with which
> young women in America contrive to manage their thoughts
> and their language amid all the difficulties of free conversa-
> tion.
>
> In France, where traditions of every age are still so
> strangely mingled in the opinions and tastes of the people,
> women commonly receive a reserved, retired, and almost
> conventual education, as they did in aristocratic times; and
> then they are suddenly abandoned without a guide and
> without assistance in the midst of all the irregularities
> inseparable from democratic society.
>
> The Americans are more consistent. Instead of inculcat-
> ing mistrust of herself, they constantly seek to enhance
> her confidence in her own strength of character. Far from
> hiding the corruptions of the world from her, they prefer
> that she should see them at once and train herself to shun
> them.
>
> Although the Americans are a very religious people, they
> do not rely on religion alone to defend the virtue of woman;
> they seek to arm her reason also.
>
> I am aware that an education of this kind is not without
> danger; I am sensible that it tends to invigorate the judgment
> at the expense of the imagination and to make cold and
> virtuous women instead of affectionate wives and agreeable
> companions to man. Society may be more tranquil and better
> regulated, but domestic life has often fewer charms. These,
> however, are secondary evils, which may be braved for
> the sake of higher interests. At the stage at which we are
> now arrived, the choice is no longer left to us; a democratic
> education is indispensable to protect women from the

dangers with which democratic institutions and manners surround them.

Seminaries

At about the time that public schools were becoming coeducational, a "seminary movement," led by Catharine Beecher and Emma Willard, established a series of schools for women, mainly in New England. The schools were modeled on the English finishing schools for girls. They were generally chartered by the state and privately endowed when funds were available. A seminary at Troy, New York, was founded in 1821 by Emma Willard, and one in Hartford, Connecticut, in 1824 by Catharine Beecher. Their purpose was to teach religious, moral, literary, domestic, and ornamental education.

Catharine Beecher had attended—for six years, starting at age ten—one of the first schools for girls, Miss Pierce's Academy at Litchfield, Connecticut. After the death of her husband, she set up her own school in Hartford and later became involved in both the normal school and the common school movements, as did other of her associates in the seminary movement. These seminaries tended increasingly to teach substantive academic subjects including math, philosophy, and science, along with the usual offerings in the arts.

Frederick Marryat, a British writer, traveled by steamboat up the Hudson River to Albany, where he stopped to visit the Albany Female Academy founded in 1814. About this visit, in about 1837, he wrote:

> Here again is a rivalry between Albany and Troy, each of them glorying in possessing the largest seminary for the education of young ladies, who are sent from every State of the Union, to be finished off at one or the other of them.
>
> Conceive three hundred modern Portias, who regularly take their degrees, and emerge from the portico of the seminary full of algebra, equality, and the theory of the

constitution! The quantity and variety crammed into them
is beyond all calculation.

Under a certain age girls are certainly much quicker
than boys, and I presume would retain what they learnt
if it were not for their subsequent duties in making puddings,
and nursing babies. Yet there are affairs which must be
performed by one sex or the other, and of what use can
algebra and other abstruse matters be to a woman in her
present state of domestic thralldom.

Normal Schools and Common Schools

These seminaries helped to train a pool of teachers
for the common schools that were experiencing such
a rapid growth at the time. People like Calvin Stowe
and Horace Mann supported the seminary movement
as they actively led the common school movement
which sought free, compulsory public education. Thus
were combined the struggle for the common school
and the struggle for the advancing education of women.

In 1837 Catharine Beecher left the schools she had
founded to become a full-time advocate of both normal
schools for women (to train them for teaching) and
public schools for both sexes. With the help of Horace
Mann and others, she campaigned to open the profession of teaching to women. The National Board of
Popular Education, established by Catharine Beecher,
placed more than 400 Eastern women in teaching
positions in the new Western schools. Teaching became the legitimation for women's entry into higher
education.

The first normal school for women only was opened
in 1839 in Lexington, Massachusetts. Until the time
of the Civil War, only about fourteen normal schools
existed. The Civil War stimulated their rapid growth,
and by 1872 more than a hundred normal schools
had been established. By 1917 there were 234 public
normal schools, the women in them outnumbering
men by about ten to one.

Women were hired as teachers in large part because

their labor was cheaper. In Maine in the mid-nineteenth century, male teachers worked for about $15
a month, and women teachers for less than $5.

By 1890, about two out of every three teachers were
women. The opening of teaching as a profession for
women virtually transformed the education of women.
Before that time, the professions and the colleges that
trained for the professions had been closed to them.
The participation of women in the professions and
in higher education spread from their attendance at
normal schools and their dominance in the teaching
profession.

After the Civil War, secondary schools had spread
rapidly, and by 1890 about twice as many girls as
boys were graduating from high school. The Civil
War brought many opportunities for women, not the
least of them the opportunity to teach in the free
coeducational primary and secondary schools that had
become common throughout the nation.

Colleges

Oberlin became the first coeducational college in
1833, and Antioch the second, twenty years later. Utah
was the first of the state universities to admit women
(1850) and Florida, Georgia, and Virginia the last.
(In England, Oxford did not grant degrees to women
until 1920, and not until then were women admitted
to the legal profession.)

In 1861 the first woman's college, Vassar, was
founded, including at its core the daily and systematic
study of the holy scriptures. Also offered were scientific and classical courses, the latter including large
doses of Ovid, Terence, Horace, Cicero, Homer,
Euripides, Plato, and Aristotle.

The early records of Oberlin suggest that women,
in their first college experience, were unable to pursue
the same courses of study as males. They were often
required to wash the clothes of male students, wait
on them at meals, and clean their rooms. When Lucy

Stone graduated from Oberlin she refused to write
a graduation essay because women were not permitted
to read such essays aloud at graduation. A male could,
however, read aloud the essays that women had written.

The plan for Oberlin, originated by a Presbyterian
pastor, was designed to serve both sexes as well as
both white and black races. Its departments included
Preparatory, Teachers, Collegiate, and Theological.
The college was designed, above all, to provide a
substan_ial education at the lowest possible rates, and
all students were required to engage in manual labor
four hours daily as a means of self-support.

English author Sophia Jex Blake visited Oberlin
College in 1865, at a time when many of the students
were Civil War veterans of somewhat uncouth manners. Oberlin students at that time numbered more
than 900, about half male and half female. "Colored"
students, varying widely in hue, formed about a third
of the student body. Miss Blake reports that she heard
with great interest that in the year of her visit, only
one woman graduated, a "colored" girl, originally a
slave, who had not even then paid her full ransom
to her former owners.

The full college course was taken by fewer women
than men. The Ladies Course was designed for those
who wanted a substantial education but did not wish
to graduate from the college.

Miss Blake writes about the Preparatory Department,
which prepared for entrance to the College:

> It was a very curious sight to go into the recitation-rooms,
> and see some benches filled with young men 'bearded like
> pards,' and others with young women of corresponding age,
> many of them of different shades of 'color,' labouring
> painfully at the elements of grammar or geography, under
> the auspices of some young undergraduate (more often a
> woman than a man), often much their junior; while side
> by side with them would sit, perhaps, children of twelve

or fourteen, their equals in book-learning, if in nothing
else.

Men and women occupied separate boarding halls but
met for joint meals. Recitations began after breakfast at
8 a.m. and continued until noon. All games of chance or
skill were prohibited, including chess.

The general average of Oberlin students may, perhaps,
be most fairly compared to that of government students
in our training colleges, and yet the comparison is very
inadequate, for they represent here the whole of society,
and not a single class.

In two respects the roughness of manners at Oberlin
seemed greater than elsewhere: firstly, in the queer attitudes
indulged in by the students during class hours, and secondly,
in the incessant spitting that went on then as well as at
all other times. It certainly did strike one with amazement
when watching one of the recitations to see young men
with their heels poised on the back of the next seat about
on a level with their heads. . . .

This, joined to the barbarous English which is so very
general, makes it hard for a European to recognise and
allow for real scholarship beneath an exterior of person
. . . .

As a rule the girls seemed considerably more civilized
than the young men. . . .

A custom obtains here which it is hard for a stranger
to admire, viz. the opening of *every* recitation with either
a hymn or a prayer. . . . The first time I was present on
such an occasion was at the lecture on physiology. The
names were called; instantly on the conclusion of the list
some one struck up, 'All hail the power of Jesu's Name'
. . . and the lecturer began briskly, 'What did I say were
the physical functions?'

It is the education alone which is common to both sexes,
the social life being completely separate, with the exception
that the meals are shared. At prayer-meetings, indeed, all
the students may meet, and at the different lectures in the
chapel, as well as all recitations in the classrooms; but they
are strictly forbidden to walk to and from such meetings
with those of the opposite sex, or to have any intercourse
with them out of hours.

In the classrooms the girls generally occupy the front

benches, and the young men those behind, or sometimes one side of the room is appropriated to each, as in the chapel a general division runs down the middle.

The first advantage of the system is its economy, the provision requisite for educating the youth of one sex being, as is urged, usually sufficient for both. . . . It is, I suppose, undeniable, that where provision for educating both sexes is not made, it is the girls that will go to the wall, as is seen almost everywhere in England when once we pass beyond the limit of national schools, where both sexes are more or less commonly taught together.

The next argument brought forward is the mutually beneficial effect which is likely to be exercised by male and female students when brought together for the purposes of study. 'That society is most happy,' says the pamphlet, 'which conforms most strictly to the order of nature as indicated in the family relation, where brother and sister mutually elevate and restrain each other.'

'A more correct idea of the character of the female sex' is another advantage to be expected by young men under such a system. . . . By isolating women from men, moreover, they may be made into prudes, on the one hand; or, 'snatching the boon of education which should have been freely bestowed,' they may, on the other, become really and offensively masculine from the very position of antagonism into which they find themselves forced.

The Professor of Greek told me that he was unable to see much difference between the students of the two sexes: 'But for the difference in sound of voice, I should find it hard, or impossible, with my eyes shut, to tell one from the other.'

The Professor of Mathematics . . . 'I have found the work done by ladies to be fully equal to that of the gentlemen—*fully;* and it has more than once occurred that the best scholar in my class was a lady.'

After the Civil War, following the example of Oberlin, even the older and more established colleges became coeducational, so that by 1880 half of all colleges in the country were coeducational.

Strong sentiment still existed for the exclusion of women from the more elite private colleges. In 1873,

Edward H. Clarke, former Harvard professor, was still arguing publicly that education would strain the minds of women beyond their capacities and make them physiologically unfit for household roles.

The conspicuous academic success of women in the first women's colleges that offered the bachelor's degree (Elmira, Vassar, Ingham, Rutgers Female College—and later Smith, Wellesley, Bryn Mawr, Barnard, and Radcliffe) demonstrated the academic competence of women, while the dramatic spurt in their college enrollments demonstrated their eagerness for education. The "bachelor's" degree became coeducational.

While American elite colleges borrowed heavily from their British counterparts, the common schools borrowed heavily from Prussian models, at least in their scope and their organizational structure.

Prussia was the first state to adopt a system of universal public education, beginning at roughly the same time that military service was made universal and compulsory throughout Prussia. Both served the same purpose: the advancement of Prussian military power. Universal education provided a base for literacy, discipline, cultural integration, and nationalist sentiment which contributed to the swift rise of the Prussian military state. Since women played no role in the military or in the affairs of state, they were generally segregated or subordinated in the educational system.

In Prussia, females were excluded from the universities and from the secondary Gymnasien and Realschulen until late in the nineteenth century. Even in the Volksschulen, the elementary "folkschools," boys and girls were educated separately except in places where separate schools could not be maintained. Private schools provided various types of secondary education for girls, but not until almost the twentieth century did any of these schools adopt the classical studies that qualified students for admission to the universities. In 1900 there were several Gymnasien

for girls. These led to teacher training. programs for
secondary school teachers and later to admission into
certain departments of the university. Advanced and
integrated education for women lagged rather far
behind the American model.

The successes of the Prussian system of universal
education led to the adoption of similar systems in
other parts of the western world, including the United
States. The motives for such emulation was not wholly
the desire to be competitive militarily and commer-
cially. In the United States, it was inspired also by
egalitarian sentiments, a democratic ideology, the need
for an educated work force, and, in the case of women,
the growing awareness of their social contribution as
well as the need to provide professional jobs for them.
The coeducational school, with females occupying a
status in it that was more nearly equal than subordinate,
became the prototype of American education.

The common school movement was actively supported by liberated women of the day, including
seminary women, not only because universal education
would include girls along with boys, but also because
the proliferation of public schools would provide
highly desirable jobs for all the women who were
beginning to emerge from the seminaries, colleges,
and normal schools. Women became teachers. It was
their first giant stride toward occupational liberation.

Sexual Democracy and Discrimination

6

Male Dominance and School Leadership

Probably the chief source of inequality in elementary and secondary education is found not in the classroom but in the fact that administration and school leadership at all levels has been dominated by males. School administration, local and state boards of education, the U.S. Office of Education, the National Education Association, the American Federation of Teachers, administration and governing boards in higher education, and virtually all groups that make or affect policy in the elementary and secondary schools, are overwhelmingly led and staffed at the highest levels by males. Among the leadership of these policy-making groups women are present only in token numbers or at relatively low policy levels.

The problem is much larger than that, however. The highest policy-making bodies in our society do not comprise the people who head and make the important operating decisions for schools. The highest level policy makers are to be found in the political and economic bodies of the society, and among those who direct these institutions. In a sense, the schools and school administration and leadership simply reflect policy that is made in city councils, state legislatures, congress, the mayors', governors', and president's offices, by the court system, and by employers and the holders of economic wealth and power. The military, even more than other powerful institutions, has also been a male preserve at top policy levels.

These political and economic institutions have been and are almost totally dominated by males. Economic institutions and corporate policy are especially exclusive male preserves. In a society such as ours, where wealth and economic power are privately held and only minimally influenced by government, the all-male exclusivity of this economic elite has certain inevitable consequences for women. Unfortunately, no attempt has been made to examine the effects of sex discrimination at these high policy levels. The problem here is probably one of access and awareness. In general, the more access women have to policy levels within a social institution, the more aware they tend to be of sex discrimination. Hence, the schools and educational systems have come under examination largely because they *are* to some extent accessible to women. Corporate and economic elites are inaccessible.

In the long run, the efforts of women to share policy making and power in the schools and other social institutions must eventually confront the formidable barriers to sexual democracy that are present at these high policy levels. They must ask, in effect, why there are so few women in congress or in governors' offices, why there have never been any women on the U.S. Supreme Court, why there are no women on the General Motors board of directors, and a host of other questions aimed at understanding how the political and economic institutions of the society are run and why women are excluded from high policy levels in them.

To say that these questions must eventually be addressed is not at all to say that the importance of sex bias in educational institutions should in any way be diminished or neglected while other questions are pursued. It is only to say that, insofar as schools prepare for adult vocations, advocate an egalitarian ideology, and reflect the patterns of dominance in the larger society, they are inextricably linked to the society for

which they are educating and preparing students.
Women have considerable leverage in educational
institutions, because of their massive presence there
as teachers and students and as opinion makers in
academia, so their attention can quite legitimately be
turned first to the question of male dominance in these
educational institutions. Perhaps the sexual democratization of the schools will provide a platform from
which women can then move toward the sexual democratization of economic and political institutions.

The Schools

Of the two omnipresent sex stereotypes in school
and society—one of the dominant male, and the other
of the natural division of labor between homemaker
and worker—the former is undoubtedly the more
damaging to the ideal of sexual democracy. It is more
damaging because it conditions the division-of-labor
stereotype. "Males are dominant, males are and should
be the leaders of everything, therefore males have and
should have all the 'good' (most rewarding, prestigeful,
powerful) jobs." And, of course, if males make all
the important decisions, they can make whatever
decisions they wish about the employment and education of women.

Male dominance in school leadership ensures that:
Males make almost all the important decisions in the
school system, decisions that undoubtedly perpetuate
and extend sex stereotypes and inequalities; Women
by their exclusion are denied vocational opportunities
and access to the high prestige and high salary jobs
for which many are qualified; The most damaging
of all sex stereotypes, that only males are capable of
high level leadership, is thereby confirmed in the
minds of the young and of the general public. Both
males and females are socialized by school and society
to believe in and advocate male dominance. Certainly
the almost total dominance of educational leadership

by males makes a large contribution to such invidious stereotyping of sex roles.

While more than two-thirds of elementary and secondary school teachers are women, only about 15 percent of principals and only about half of 1 percent of superintendents are women. Of the ninety women who were school superintendents in 1971, only two were in districts with more than 10,000 students.

Most of the few women administrators are found in elementary schools, where their numbers have been declining. In 1971, about 19 percent of elementary school principals were women, but less than 4 percent of junior high and 3 percent of senior high school principals were women.

Women are even a minority among assistant administrators, with only 34 percent of elementary school assistant principalships in 1971, and only 7 percent of deputy, associate, or assistant superintendencies.

The Fleischmann Commission report on the New York State educational system found that almost all senior administrative posts in the system were held by men and that nothing in their studies had convinced them that males were inherently superior to females as educational administrators. They concluded that the *de facto* discrimination against women was totally unjustifiable.

Participation of women in school administration has been limited in large part by the failure of training institutions to admit or recruit women into masters and doctoral programs in educational administration. Women received only about 25 percent of the masters degrees in educational administration in 1968-69, and only about 10 percent of the doctorates. It is from among these degree holders that school administrators are usually chosen.

So completely male dominated has educational leadership been that about 98 percent of all faculty in college and university educational administration departments in 1971–72 were male.

Because they are less likely than males to receive financial aid for graduate studies, women are also less likely to enter graduate programs in education that might qualify them for educational leadership. Women constituted only 32 percent of students funded by the Elementary and Secondary Education Act research training fellowship program in 1969-70, and only 12 percent of the National Defense Education Act fellows in 1961-62. Requirements by both colleges and aid granting agencies that graduates attend school full time make it difficult for women with family responsibilities to qualify for admission and aid in graduate programs.

Women school administrators earn much less than male administrators. According to the 1970 Census, the mean earnings of male superintendents was $13,500 and of women $8,700.

The same pattern of male dominance is found among other school administrators, in state and federal departments of education, and elsewhere.

The chief administrative officer in education, the U.S. Commissioner of Education, was a male in 1972, and in most other years. So were all his deputies, associates, and assistants—except two. Of the four people in the top government grade (Grade 18) of the U.S. Office of Education, none were women. Two of thirteen Grade 17 positions were held by women, one of thirty-five Grade 16 positions, twenty-three of the almost 300 Grade 15 positions, and fourteen of the almost 500 Grade 14 positions. The average grade of women in the U.S. Office of Education was Grade 7. For men it was Grade 14.

Only three state departments of education (Montana, Wisconsin, Guam) were headed by women in 1972.

Males are dominant even in the leadership of teacher organizations, although women far outnumber males in the ranks of these organizations. Males head both the American Federation of Teachers, the teacher's union, which has more than a quarter of a million members, and the National Education Association, with more than 1.3 million members. Not only are the national offices of these organizations dominated by males, the state and local offices are also. In one recent year, none of the fifty state executive secretaries of the NEA were women, although about a third of the presidents were women. Only a few of the state heads of the AFT are women. Of the professional staffs employed by these two organizations, less than a quarter are women.

Males dominate the field of educational research and the American Educational Research Association, the major professional association of educational researchers. Until 1973, Phi Delta Kappa, one of the largest and most influential of professional organizations in education, was an exclusive "professional fraternity for men in education," dedicated to the promotion of leadership in education.

As for citizen leadership in education, only 20 percent of the members of local school boards in the country are women. These local school boards hire and fire superintendents, raise money for the schools in many cases, and have considerable influence on educational policy and the administration of schools. Women are more active in parent-school organizations than males, although the rates of participation have not been calculated, (nor has their role in the leadership of parent groups), but in their roles as citizens and parents they are far less likely than males to occupy leadership roles in the schools.

7

Socialization, Sex Roles, Discrimination

A vast, almost staggering, body of research has accumulated on the early socialization of females and males and the ways in which they learn adult sex roles and make career choices. Obviously the home and school have important influences on these choices, although other influences may also be felt, including peers, the mass media, reading material, and indeed virtually all experiences the young have. Presumably the home and school have most influence, since their major function is to socialize and guide the young.

Research tends to support the common sense assumption that parents and the role models and guidance they offer children have a more significant impact on sex-role learning than do other influences.

Girls are likely to accept their mothers' views of what behaviors, attitudes, aspirations are appropriately female. They may also model their behavior and career choices on their fathers if they have close and admiring relations with them.

One study, reported in *Scientific American,* of wives of graduate students in the Boston area found, for example, that an important predictor of a woman's female-role ideology (the extent to which she sought gratification through her own achievement) is her perception of her mother's satisfaction with life. Dissatisfied mothers in male-dominated households tended to produce daughters who wished to achieve on their own rather than vicariously.

Researchers have been especially interested in why some girls make nontraditional career choices or prefer a career to housewifery. Again they find that girls tend to derive their nontraditional choices from their parents or their family situation.

Much less is known about the influence of schools on sex-role learning and career choices, although speculation and research on the subject are hardly lacking. Such inquiries must inevitably deal with two aspects of school instruction: what the schools teach boys and girls about sex roles and career choices, and what effect such instruction actually has on students.

It is a relatively simple matter, for example, to determine what kinds of career guidance and career goals schools transmit to females, and it is usually easy also to determine whether or not the schools, by means overt or subtle, guide females into domestic roles and submissive and nonassertive behavior. What is far more difficult to determine is the actual *effect* such teaching may have on the sex-role learning of girls.

The schools, for instance, may provide students with sex-stereotyped reading materials. The extent to which this is done is verifiable. Much less ascertainable is the effect these materials have on the sex-role behavior of girls and boys.

My own hypothesis, perhaps an unprovable one, is that sex-role socialization in the *primary* school tends to be sex neutral in its effects if not in the chief aspects of its practice. The exceptions are the forms of sex-segregated instruction (in physical education, shop, homemaking) that schools have carried on and that are now virtually outlawed.

What is most important for sex-role learning in the public primary school is that the course of study is standardized and classrooms are fully integrated. Boys and girls sit with each other in a random mixture, they study the same materials, and they are taught by the same teachers, most of whom are female.

Beyond that, the stereotyping of female sex and career roles either in texts or teacher behavior is discriminatory and lamentable where it occurs, but perhaps not very influential. What is probably far more important than the number of male pronouns and active male images in texts and tests are the opportunities that schools, and especially higher education and the job market, either open or close to female students and career aspirants. The sex roles that girls learn and the career choices they make are far more responsive to the opportunity structure of schools and the working world than they are to whatever hidden persuaders are present in school readers. Indeed, women have taken on new occupational roles and new views of women's sex roles because they have been offered, and have made for themselves, new options outside the home. The change is not a response to changes in texts and tests, for there has been no such change.

It is not usually until secondary school that differential curriculum opportunities are available to males and females. The course of study is no longer standardized as in the primary school. Where there was only one road, in the secondary school there are many. Girls may be advised by counselors to enter a commercial rather than a college curriculum in the high school. Boys may be advised to pursue science, math, or technical courses in preparation for professional occupations. Girls may be excluded (as they have been in New York City and elsewhere) from the most elite schools of science, trade-technology, or academic studies. Girls may be dissuaded from assuming positions of organizational leadership and dominance. Boys may be encouraged, and girls discouraged, from participating in team sports.

It may be fair to say, however, that even in secondary schools, females are in a position of greater equality in relation to males than they are in higher education or in institutions outside the school. To say that is not to minimize the importance of stereotyping and discrimination that are present, but only to put such practices in perspective. Sex stereotyping clearly has no more place in the schools than racial, religious, or other damaging forms of stereotyping. It is necessary not only to enumerate the occurrences of such stereotyping but also to establish a priority of importance among them.

The major discriminatory practices of elementary and secondary schools, aside from the aggravated pattern of male dominance in them, are probably to be found mainly in the school's failure to encourage qualified female students to pursue studies and careers in nontraditional areas, such as science, math, technology, and in the outright exclusion of females, at least in the past, from schools and courses of study that have been available to males.

The school's failure has its source mainly in the desire realistically to reflect the opportunities and occupations available to women. Rather than advancing the idea of equal opportunity into the working world, it has tended to lag behind the availability of job opportunities made possible by the Civil Rights Act. In this respect, schools have not even kept pace with the changing *status quo.*

Omissions in Schools

While the public school tends to be neutral in its sex-role socialization of females, its practices can be faulted perhaps more on its omissions than its commissions. That is, the school fails to provide special guidance and resources for girls, to balance the stereotyping that occurs in the home and the nonschool world. Both the advocates of women's studies and the proponents of consciousness raising have recognized that females need special attention to balance the discriminatory practices of the past. They need more experience in working with and relating to others of their sex, for purposes of group self-awareness and advancement and more of the kind of team work and peer group experiences that boys receive in athletic and other activities. They may need special assertiveness training, more opportunities for leadership, more awareness of their almost reflexive reference to males as authority figures.

Like blacks and other minorities, they also need role models and examples of success in nontraditional activities, with models drawn from history and from contemporary society. As it is, and as even the history of women and schools reflects, history is written largely by and about males. Women play almost no role in it, except as Faerie Queenes and Egyptian *femmes fatales.* Thorough records of daily life, occupations, domestic duties, political and creative activities in which women have participated through the ages have yet to be extracted from the documents of the past and placed before the female student as proof that her sex is part of the living human record.

Moreover, in fairness to the majority of women who choose domestic roles (and to the males who might choose them), some optional instruction in family and community-related studies might suitably become a more significant part of the secondary school curriculum. Such studies would differ markedly, however, from the traditional home economics courses which often teach virtually obsolete skills, such as sewing and dressmaking. Family studies might include explorations of consumer issues, household management and investment, creative cooking, health foods and nutrition, child rearing and, beyond that, community and political activities. The neglect of such studies, except in traditional home economics courses and quickie family education classes, indicates the extent to which public schools have gone in trying to neutralize the effect of domestic sex-role stereotypes. Males should, of course, be encouraged to participate in such courses along with women, as they are in Swedish schools.

The stereotyping of adult work-and-domestic roles has served to constrict the options of males at least as much as those of females. Women have learned that they may choose between work and homemaking. Males have been offered no such option, although in many cases homemaking is clearly preferable to the work options that are available to them.

The socialization of women often leads them to satisfy vicariously whatever needs for achievement and recognition they have. They live through others—their husbands and children in the family setting, or their bosses, patients, or others, in the work setting. They forego achievement themselves in order to serve others and help them achieve, and their gratification comes through association with persons of recognized status. So traditional has the role of silent partner become in this country that the wives of successful men in politics and business have come to have a recognized, public status of their own, much as the manager of a baseball team might have. The wives of such men become public figures and are often required themselves to pass job screening tests to which their husbands are subjected. It is a special status, enjoyed almost exclusively by American women, indicating perhaps that their partnership with their males, through whom they live vicariously, is one of greater equality than it is in other countries.

Most women enjoy no such public status, however. Certainly the altruism which is part of their vicarious gratification is a quality that can not be oversupplied in any society. Still, it is demonstrably possible for women to mix the sources of gratification they achieve without damage to themselves or others, and more often to the benefit of all. Just as a mother and wife can easily feed herself to her own taste, while feeding her family to their taste, so can she easily gratify her own need for recognition, at the same time as she assists and enjoys the achievements of significant others. Developing both sources of gratification is part of the ambivalence in the role of women, but with the aid of suitable counseling and school experiences, this role strain might be reduced. The tendency to subordination, in this and other respects, has undoubtedly been a major barrier to the achievement of equal social status for women.

Women who seek career rather than homemaking roles tend to be high achievers with a high need for achievement. Mothers with a career orientation tend to produce daughters with a career orientation. High levels of parental education, career-oriented mothers, closeness of parents and child, some positive identification with father, all tend to influence daughters to pursue careers. Also of considerable influence is the female's perception of the male attitude toward career women. If she expects conflict with men, or with her husband, she tends to forego a career. The literature on socialization has dealt with women's and men's views of the ideal woman. Women, it is found, tend to think men prefer passive women, but men claim that they prefer active and assertive women to those who are passive and submissive. Greater clarification of these preferences is needed, since females tend to model their behavior so much on the preferences of males.

Texts and Tests

Both the texts and the standardized tests that schools use make far more references to boys than to girls. They also tend to stereotype sex roles: boys are leaders, active, courageous; girls are mothers, helpful, subordinate.

In preparing the *American Heritage Dictionary*, for example, a thousand of the most used publications in schools around the country were examined. A computer analysis of 10,000 samples from this material showed clear evidence of a male orientation in the

material. The words "girl" or "girls" appeared 2,200
times, and the words "boy" or "boys" 4,700 times.
Moreover, thirteen of the twenty first names that
occurred most frequently were male.

Another study of junior high school science and
math texts found that noted female scientists and
mathematicians were ignored and that illustrations and
problems contained numerous sex stereotypes. Girls
cooked and sewed, and boys did construction work
and engaged in sports.

Dick and Jane as Victims, a study in New Jersey
schools of 134 books published by eighteen different
textbook companies, found that male biographies outnumbered female by six to one. Women were portrayed
in 25 occupations, men in 147, and female occupations
were mainly traditional ones: teacher, nurse, office
worker. In roles requiring ingenuity or bravery, males
outnumbered girls by four to one.

Sex stereotyping is also extremely common in television, to which the young are exposed for periods often
as lengthy as the school day. Even programs such
as "Sesame Street" introduced female characters only
under pressure from women's groups—stereotyped
characters to be sure.

Popular child development and child rearing books
have also contained stereotypes, most notably the
works of Dr. Benjamin Spock, whose views of sex
roles are illustrated in this passage:

> In bringing up our children—boys as well as girls—I
> think we should be enthusiastic about their maleness or
> femaleness as attributes to be proud of, enjoyed, emphasized,
> rather than taken for granted or even denied as they so
> often are today. A boy should know that his father enjoys
> his company in a special way because they can talk about
> cars or carpentry or sports. Even a small boy should feel
> that his mother appreciates his manly help in carrying things
> for her, opening doors, running errands, fixing things. . . .
> Most of all a girl needs a mother who shows enthusiasm

for playing the role of woman herself—with verve and style
. . . .

Most child development literature still accepts most of the gender stereotypes about appropriate behavior of females and males.

As for the more than 200 million achievement tests that are used in the country each year, one study of the major tests, including California, Iowa, Metropolitan, SRA, Stanford, found that almost all tests used more male than female nouns and pronouns and that women and men were portrayed mainly in stereotyped roles. An examination of College Entrance Examination Board material showed the same pattern.

Sports

Athletic programs and health education classes, because they rarely involve academic studies, may be viewed as matters of relatively minor importance. Such views neglect the significant socializing effect that sports have on young people. Often they provide the chief means of gender socialization within the school. In team sports especially, males learn to cooperate, organize their activities, work harmoniously with other males, play to win, and in doing so, they often form close peer groups that set standards for male behavior and exclude females from group membership. Girls have generally been denied such socializing experiences. As a result, they tend to be less responsive to group behavior, more fragmented, less able to act with other females on behalf of their own interests. Boys develop a male bond through sports; girls seldom do.

Moreover, public schools generally have spent far more money on recreational and athletic activity for boys than for girls. In secondary schools the discrepancy is often almost ten to one in favor of boys. In public colleges and universities, large sums of money are spent on scholarships, travel, stadiums, dormitories, allowances for male athletes, while only miniscule sums have been spent for female athletes.

Title IX of the Education Act of 1972 is expected to have a dramatic impact on athletic programs at all educational levels, especially in correcting the imbalance in expenditures for male and female sports.

Whether greater participation in team sports can provide peer group socializing which will resemble what boys achieve through sports and other peer activities remains to be seen. What is apparent is that males learn a variety of gender-related activity in the peer group, such as risk-taking, assertiveness, bonding, collective behavior, mobility of movement, emotional coolness, dominance, self-defense (and offense), manual and physical skills. If girls cannot acquire such behavior, at least in modified form, in peer and play groups, then other efforts may be required to supply the deficiency. Certainly schools do not now teach either girls or boys, in regular academic courses, the value of courage, assertiveness, collective behavior, or teamwork.

Counseling

Vocational counseling is often guided by personality and interest inventories, tests that link certain personality traits and interests with vocations suitable to those characteristics. If the student's responses on these tests indicate aggression and dominance, for example, the student may be counseled to enter management training where these traits would presumably be compatible with career success. Women, less likely to register dominant traits on these tests, may be advised not to enter management careers, even where strong interest is present.

The net effect of the use of these tests in the schools and elsewhere is to direct males and females into sex-stereotyped occupations and away from atypical occupations, even when these personality traits are not qualifications for the jobs.

Most students consult school counselors about their career plans, and in most cases it is the counselor who suggests the vocational choice. It has been found that counselors are generally unaware of the sex bias in vocational inventories, that they themselves have strong preferences for traditional male and female occupations, and that when a student selects a non-traditional career goal, they are likely to recommend additional counseling. On many of the vocational tests, women who choose male occupations are labeled deviant, or they may be labeled masculine. Quite naturally, girls are not eager to acquire these labels.

Tests used most often in vocational counseling are the Kuder Preference Record and the Strong Vocational Interest Blanks. These tests have had different scales for males and females, with scores reported separately by sex. Jobs such as carpenter, contractor, auto sales-man are included on the male form and items such as beauty specialist, dental assistant, artists' model appear only on the female form. This has meant that women could not choose to be auto salesmen and men could not choose to be beauty specialists. The Strong test has been revised and now uses only one questionnaire, but it still uses separate scoring and norms, so that a girl who indicates interest in becoming an auto sales(man) will learn that she is deviant from the female norm.

Researchers using the Strong test have had much more success with men than with women. The job categories on the form for females have been much more limited than on the form for males, since the traditional female jobs have been much fewer in number than male jobs. The form was first used to predict career choices for males, and it was rather successful in doing that. Men tended to enter the careers that the test indicated they were suited for. It was found, however, that the women's form could not predict career choice for women.

The manual for the Strong test states:

Many young women do not appear to have strong
occupational interests, and they may score high only in
certain 'premarital' occupations: elementary school teacher,
office worker, stenographer-secretary.

Such a finding is disappointing to many college women,
since they are likely to consider themselves career-oriented.
In such cases, the selection of an area of training or an
occupation should probably be based upon practical consi-
derations—fields that can be pursued part-time, are easily
resumed after periods of nonemployment, are readily available in different locales.

Since the participation of women in the labor market
has grown dramatically in past decades, and since
the overwhelming majority of women will enter the
labor market for a prolonged period at some point
in their lives, quite obviously career education and
career counseling are matters of urgent concern in
the education and counseling of female students.

Vocational guidance offered in schools has not only
failed to familiarize girls with the range of career
opportunities that are possible for them; it has rein-
forced the discriminatory patterns that exist in the
job market and in school programs.

Counseling has been perhaps the least sex-neutral
aspect of primary and especially secondary schools.
In general, counseling has been an instrument for
preserving the traditional curricular and career separations between the sexes. It has not been sufficiently
aware of changing job markets, opportunities, or levels
of consciousness. Counselors have often directed girls
away from college preparatory courses and into commercial studies. They have failed to make girls aware,
for example, of the need for certain kinds of math
in professional studies—as medicine, economics, psy-
chology, sociology, and engineering.

An adequate school system of career education and
counseling would provide girls with a full range of
job experiences, with exposure to successful women
in nontraditional jobs, and to women in a variety of

occupations who successfully combine work and homemaking. It would keep abreast of the legal status of women with respect to work and education, and it would be prepared to inform students of specific occupations, employers, and training programs that have been, or could be, opened to women.

Such a system would also include communications with parents and their counseling, since the career orientation of girls is so largely derived from parental influences.

8

Higher Education

The most serious cases of sex segregation and discrimination in the schools are found in higher education. Indeed, more charges of sex discrimination have been brought against colleges and universities than against any other institution.

Discrimination here is more pervasive and the stakes are much higher than at other school levels. Higher education has an extremely important sorting-and-selecting function. It selects students for leadership roles and occupational rewards in the society, and so has the power to open or bar the way to vocational and professional opportunities for women.

Discrimination in higher education has taken various forms. Women have been excluded from many elite schools. They have also been excluded from, or discriminated against, in admission to many colleges and professional training programs. Counseling services have often directed them into only the most traditional occupations. Guidance programs have failed to inform women students of the variety of occupational and educational opportunities. Women students have been excluded from, and discriminated against, in recreational and athletic programs. Scholarship and financial aid programs have favored males. Curriculum content has largely been shaped by and for males. Successful role models are not as often provided for female students, since the highest ranking faculty members and administrators have been overwhelmingly male. Moreover, colleges have failed to offer class scheduling

that would better suit the needs of women with
household responsibilities, and most universities have
failed to create special programs for mature women
on their reentry into the labor market.

The college years cover a span of time when women
are most likely to begin raising families and when
it is most difficult for them to take on full educational
commitments. Insofar as higher education has failed
to adapt to the scheduling needs of women—by flexible scheduling, early admissions, substitution of exams
and experience for class attendance, provision of day-
care facilities, etc.—it has in fact limited female
participation.

Discrimination in higher education is to some extent
a continuation of what is found in incipient form in
the elementary and secondary school—that is, sex
stereotypes with respect to authority and leadership
roles. Insofar as males are believed to be more suited
for leadership, positions of authority, and dominant
roles—in the school administration, top elected student office, etc.—both males and females are socialized
to the acceptance of these stereotypes in higher education. At the college level, these stereotypes take on
their most serious and damaging form. It is there that
biased attitudes are turned into discrimination.

The consequence of such sex stereotypes and discrimination is that only 39 percent of women high
school graduates went to college in 1972—compared
with 53 percent of male high school graduates. Large
numbers of highly qualified women are prevented
from using their full capabilities. It is estimated, for
example, that about nine in ten qualified students who
do not go to college are women. Many of these are
working-class women whose entrance to college is
limited by high college costs and the difficulties of
earning tuition money. In the lowest socioeconomic
groups, 24 percent fewer women enter college than
do their male counterparts.

In 1972, among first-time college students, 50 percent of women were in the top quarter of their high school class, 32 percent in the second quarter, 16 percent in the third, and 2 percent in the fourth. Males were placed much lower in their high school classes. Thirty-eight percent of these first-time college males were in the top quarter, 34 percent in the second, 24 in the third, and 4 percent in the fourth quarter of their classes.

Yet of these entering students, 11 percent of males and 7 percent of females planned to get a Ph.D. or Ed.D.; 10 percent of males and 4 percent of females planned on getting a medical degree; and 7 percent of males and 2 percent of females planned on getting a law degree. Thus, the core of female students who aspire to the most advanced levels of education is already limited at the time of entry into college. The experiences of women during their college life even further reduce that core.

Admissions

College admissions practices, especially in elite and religious schools, have openly discriminated against women. Schools have set quotas on women students, admitting only a designated proportion into the total class. Many others (including, in the past, the New York City colleges) have required of women higher grade point averages or test scores at the time of admission. Even public colleges with the most venerable and publicized egalitarian traditions have discriminated against women in admissions.

At the University of Michigan, for example, the admissions office had "adjusted" requirements during the sixties to insure that more males than females would be admitted, though more qualified females (in test scores and grades) applied for admission. Pennsylvania State University maintained an arbitrary ratio of 2.5 men to each female admitted. At Stanford's graduate school, one in every 2.8 men who applied was admitted, but only one in every 4.7 female applicants, though

more females than males were qualified according to
Stanford's standards.

Even in public institutions, supported by female
as well as male taxpayers, admissions officers have
not been held accountable for their admissions practices. The arbitrary quotas and other devices used by
these officers (most of whom are male), in collaboration
with top male administrators, has been challenged in
the courts in recent years only.

Subtle forms of selectivity and discrimination continue. A national study of admission practices of 240
colleges in 1971, for example, found that when entrance qualifications were equal, colleges more often
accepted the male applicants.

Enrollments and Degrees

Despite these admissions practices and other difficulties, college enrollments of women are, and have
been for some time, a large proportion of total enrollments in bachelors' and masters' programs, but not
at the doctoral level. The ratio of males to females
enrolled in college has changed little in the past
forty-five years. Females are, and have been for at
least that period, about 40 percent of all college
enrollments. More than three million American women
now attend college, a number larger than the entire
combined populations of Alaska, Delaware, Nevada,
New Hampshire, Vermont, and Wyoming.

Of college degree recipients, the proportion of
women has risen significantly since 1900, from about
20 percent to about 40 percent of the total. Since about
1930, the proportion has held fairly constant, though
it dipped somewhat during the post World War II
years, when males, using the GI Bill, enrolled in
colleges in large numbers. Aside from that period,
the proportion of females among college students has
not changed much in almost half a century.

While the proportion of female recipients of both

bachelor's and master's degrees has remained fairly high (at about 40 percent in each case), the proportion receiving doctorates has declined. In 1930 women were about 15 percent of all recipients of doctor's degrees; by 1970 they were only 13 percent. Thus, not only are the numbers of women earning doctor's degrees relatively small, they are declining as a proportion of the whole. These numbers are strategically important for women, since it is the doctor's degree that increasingly prepares students for dominant roles and occupations in the society.

Only about 16,000 of the 166,000 students in graduate professional schools in 1969 were women. As a consequence of these under-enrollments, women are less than 4 percent of lawyers, about 7 percent of physicians, 2 percent of dentists, and 1 percent of engineers. In Sweden women are 24 percent of lawyers. In Denmark, women are 70 percent of dentists. In Britain women are 16 percent of physicians, and in Israel 24 percent.

Admissions practices in graduate departments and professional schools are even more shrouded in mystery than are the admissions practices of undergraduate schools. Similarly obscure are the specific requirements of graduation, including, in the case of the Ph.D., the unique requirements of oral examinations and dissertations.

Degrees received by women tend to be concentrated in traditional fields of study. Thirty-nine percent of women who received degrees in 1968-69 were in teacher education, 22 percent in humanities, 15 percent in social sciences, 4 percent in health professions, and 4 percent in natural sciences. This distribution has changed very little in a fifteen-year period.

About 40 percent of bachelors' degrees earned by women are in education, more than half of master's degrees, and about 30 percent of doctor's degrees. Women earn relatively few degrees in math, physical science, technological subjects, or administration.

Table 5. Earned Degrees Conferred
Earned Degrees Conferred, by Field of Study, Level of Degree, and Sex: 1970
[Includes Puerto Rico, Guam, and Virgin Islands]

Major Field of Study	Bachelor's and 1st Professional Degrees[1]			Master's			Doctorates		
	Total	Male	Female	Total	Male	Female	Total	Male	Female
All fields	833,322	486,949	346,373	209,387	126,146	83,241	29,872	25,892	3,980
Agriculture	9,192	8,712	480	1,480	1,370	110	726	698	28
Animal science	2,553	2,333	220	301	285	16	159	153	6
All other	6,639	6,379	260	1,179	1,085	94	567	545	22
Architecture[2]	3,902	3,698	204	658	615	43	11	10	1
Biological sciences	37,676	27,162	10,514	5,835	3,991	1,844	3,289	2,820	469
Premedical, predental, and preveterinary	3,015	2,757	258	(X)	(X)	(X)	(X)	(X)	(X)
Biology, general	24,598	16,970	7,628	2,589	1,756	833	471	377	94
Zoology, general	5,584	4,412	1,172	730	498	232	412	370	42
All other	4,479	3,023	1,456	2,516	1,737	779	2,406	2,073	333
Business and commerce	106,279	96,760	9,519	21,417	20,659	758	603	593	10
Accounting	21,354	19,459	1,895	1,083	1,004	79	56	53	3
General, without major specialization	52,452	48,331	4,121	13,854	13,391	463	356	351	5
All other	32,473	28,970	3,503	6,480	6,264	216	191	189	2
Computer science and systems analysis	1,544	1,345	199	1,459	1,324	135	107	105	2
Education[3]	166,423	41,604	124,819	79,841	35,696	44,145	5,894	4,698	1,196
Specialized teaching fields	68,670	30,889	37,781	21,378	9,779	11,599	1,111	846	265
General teaching fields	94,192	9,175	85,017	22,585	6,569	16,016	746	580	166
Other education fields	3,561	1,540	2,021	35,878	19,348	16,530	4,037	3,272	765
Engineering[2]	44,772	44,434	338	15,597	15,425	172	3,681	3,657	24

English and journalism	62,467	22,208	40,259	9,348	3,871	5,477	1,222	849	373
English and literature	56,508	18,675	37,833	8,486	3,310	5,176	1,205	832	373
Journalism	5,959	3,533	2,426	862	561	301	17	17	—
Fine and applied arts	35,945	15,361	20,584	7,849	4,158	3,691	734	592	142
Music³	5,433	2,424	3,009	2,130	1,128	1,002	278	237	41
Speech and dramatic arts³	10,367	4,604	5,763	2,546	1,194	1,352	301	256	45
All other	20,145	8,333	11,812	3,173	1,836	1,337	155	99	56
Foreign languages and literature	21,587	5,703	15,884	5,175	1,928	3,247	874	581	293
Forestry	2,177	2,160	17	327	316	11	97	97	—
Geography	3,747	2,945	802	637	524	113	145	140	5
Health professions	36,334	18,380	17,954	4,660	2,219	2,441	357	299	58
Dentistry, D.D.S. and D.M.D.	3,748	3,712	36	(X)	(X)	(X)	(X)	(X)	(X)
Medicine, M.D.	8,374	7,661	713	(X)	(X)	(X)	(X)	(X)	(X)
Nursing	11,280	160	11,120	1,549	18	1,531	11	1	10
Pharmacy (excl. pharmacology)	4,543	3,690	853	229	191	38	79	68	11
All other	8,389	3,157	5,232	2,882	2,010	872	267	230	37
Home economics³	10,305	290	10,015	1,297	75	1,222	116	33	83
Law, LL.B., J.D., or higher degrees	15,715	14,837	878	884	846	38	35	32	3
Library sciences	1,054	86	968	6,544	1,108	5,436	40	24	16

—Represents zero. X Not applicable.

[1] Includes first-professional degrees requiring at least 6 years.

[2] Architectural engineering included with engineering.

[3] Home economics education, music education, and speech correction included with education.

[4] Deck officer only.

Source: U.S. Office of Education, *Earned Degrees Conferred: 1969-70, Part A—Summary Data.*

A more detailed table appears in Appendix A.

Table 5.—Continued

Major Field of Study	Bachelor's and 1st Professional Degrees[1]			Master's			Doctorates		
	Total	Male	Female	Total	Male	Female	Total	Male	Female
Mathematical subjects	27,565	17,248	10,317	5,648	3,974	1,674	1,236	1,140	96
Merchant Marine[4]	233	233	—	—	—	—	—	—	—
Military, naval, or air force science	1,618	1,618	—	—	—	—	—	—	—
Philosophy	5,717	4,631	1,086	729	608	121	359	315	44
Physical sciences	21,551	18,582	2,969	5,948	5,101	847	4,313	4,077	236
Chemistry (excl. biochemistry)	11,617	9,501	2,116	2,119	1,642	477	2,167	2,000	167
Physics	5,333	5,004	329	2,205	2,047	158	1,439	1,402	37
Geology	2,255	2,011	244	567	500	67	249	242	7
All other	2,346	2,066	280	1,057	912	145	458	433	25
Psychology	33,854	19,113	14,741	4,120	2,554	1,566	1,668	1,296	372
Religion	10,957	9,102	1,855	3,184	2,403	781	405	391	14
Religious education and Bible	2,914	2,029	885	1,155	721	434	43	41	2
Theology	6,017	5,752	265	1,460	1,264	196	200	197	3
All other	2,026	1,321	705	569	418	151	162	153	9
Social sciences	155,235	97,349	57,886	23,580	15,199	8,381	3,778	3,288	490
Social sciences, general	21,021	11,381	9,640	2,092	1,359	733	48	41	7
Economics (excl. agric. econ.)	17,258	15,381	1,877	1,990	1,743	247	794	742	52
History	43,589	28,523	15,066	5,056	3,401	1,655	1,038	901	137
Political science or government	25,856	20,698	5,158	2,105	1,663	442	525	469	56
Sociology	30,848	12,445	18,403	1,816	1,139	677	534	430	104
Social work, admin., welfare	4,143	914	3,229	5,735	2,196	3,539	89	57	32
All other	12,520	8,007	4,513	4,786	3,698	1,088	750	648	102
Trade and industrial training	5,199	5,147	52	130	126	4	10	10	—
Miscellaneous	12,274	8,241	4,033	3,040	2,056	984	172	147	25

Dropout

Women graduate students are more likely than males to drop out of school because of pressures from their spouses. Twenty-one percent, or almost one in four women graduate students, drop out of school for this reason—but only 9 percent of male graduate students do.

The dropout of female students in higher education is a feature not only of discriminatory school practices but also of the tasks and obligations that are involved for many women in child rearing. Social policies directed at reducing the dropout of female college students must also, therefore, be directed at providing greater relief from these home tasks and making it easier for women to pursue college studies at home or during more flexibly scheduled hours.

As it is, among graduate students, about half of married men, and only a third of married women attend school on a full-time basis. The others are on part-time schedules.

Dedication

A Carnegie Commission study of 32,000 graduate students and faculty found that 22 percent of male and 50 percent of female sociology graduate students said that faculty do not "take female graduate students seriously." Less than 4 percent female faculty and a quarter of male faculty said "female graduate students are not as dedicated to the field as males." A quarter of male and female graduate students agreed with this statement. Obviously, there is considerable feeling among male faculty and male and female students—but not female faculty—that female graduate students are less dedicated to their studies than are males.

Leadership

A study of 376 coeducational colleges found that fewer than 5 percent of student body presidents were

women, and about 6 percent of class presidents.
Women were better represented among editors of
campus papers and yearbooks, but in roles of elected
leadership they were present in little more than token
numbers.

Women's Colleges

In academic quality, the top five women's colleges
have been rated much lower than the top five men's
colleges. In general, women's colleges have been rated
lower than either men's colleges or coeducational
colleges. Many of the women's colleges have tended
to concentrate on the humanities, the arts, and child
rearing and development, to the neglect of scientific
and technological studies. Fortunately, eroded by the
economics of school financing, the single sex college
is disappearing. In 1971, only about 16 percent of
postsecondary schools were for one sex only.

Finances

Women find it more difficult than men to finance
a college education. Fewer jobs are available to them
for part-time work. Even when they work in jobs
comparable to those of males, they tend to be paid
less. So it is that, among students not supported by
parents, 64 percent of males and only 38 percent of
females earn more than $500 during the year.

Scholarship and loan aid to students have also
favored males, especially aid administered by the
colleges themselves. While males tended to have more
funds than women, acquired from their own earnings
or from parents, far more males than females received
scholarship aid of more than $1000 a year.

Women, of course, have received much less aid from
athletic scholarships than men have. Since colleges
have refused to release this information, the exact
figures on the distribution of such aid are unknown.

At the graduate level, the result of the skewed
distribution of aid funds is that 37 percent of women

students and 49 percent of male students received aid of some kind during 1972.

The high prestige and most generous scholarships are especially likely to be awarded to males. One study shows that more than 80 percent of the most coveted scholarships go to male recipients. Fewer than 10 percent of White House Fellows or the winners of Fulbright Fellowships have been women.

Women receive on an average $518 a year in financial aid and males receive $760. Almost all federal loan and scholarship assistance is available only to full-time students, which makes it difficult for most working people and housewives to qualify under these programs. Under federal law, colleges are now required to balance the financial assistance offered to male and female students, so that aid may be more available to women in the future.

Work Roles

9

Work and Education

Instruction and Training for Women

Schools also instruct and assist women in performing a variety of roles. They can assist them as mothers by increasing the knowledge which they can then pass on to the young. They can assist them in performing their traditional homemaker roles by imparting consumer and household information and skills. They can assist them in performing their roles as citizens by providing knowledge and incentives needed to function better in their communities. They can also enrich their lives as individuals by developing their cognitive and creative powers, their interests, and their social relations. Perhaps most importantly, schools can help women to pursue their newer roles as workers by assisting in vocational guidance and preparation.

It is the latter function of education that has come under the most critical scrutiny in recent years. The education of women is closely related to their participation in the labor force. If women worked only at home, their interest in education beyond primary school would be greatly diminished and society would be less willing to support advanced education for them.

Among the nations of the world, the extent and variety of education for women has tended to vary directly with their rates of participation in the labor force. The higher the rate of participation, the longer and more diverse the education of women has tended

Table 6.   Labor Force by Sex and Years of School Completed,
1952 and 1974

	1952		1974	
	Women	Men	Women	Men
4 years of college or more	8%	8%	13%	16%
1 to 3 years of college	9%	8%	15%	15%
4 years of high school	34%	24%	44%	36%
1 to 3 years of high school	18%	19%	18%	18%
5 to 8 years of elementary school	26%	33%	9%	12%
Less than 5 years of elementary school	5%	8%	1%	2%

Note: Civilian labor force 18 years old and over in October, 1952 and 16 years old and over in March, 1974.

Women in the labor force are more likely than men to have graduated from high school, but less likely to have completed four years of college. Nearly three-quarters of women workers have high school diplomas compared to only one-half in 1952.

to be, relative to males. In a sense, then, the economic role of women has largely determined their educational experience.

The interaction between work and education has moved in both directions, however. The more education women receive, the more likely they are to press for opportunities in the working world, since education raises their occupational aspirations. It also changes their self-image, gives them leadership skills, increases their independence, and enlightens them about their human and legal rights. All of these effects of education have tended to raise the amount and the quality of the labor force experience of women.

Still, the movement of women into the labor force and their occupational advancement once they are in it, have been generated mainly by the demands of an expanding industrial market. But for these demands, the education of women would probably be far more limited than it is.

The Market

In this and similar free market societies, the demand for women workers varies greatly from time to time.

The demand has been particularly high during time of war and national need, when women have been drawn into the labor force to replace the men who are drafted into military service.

The first large-scale movement of women into the civilian labor force occurred during the Civil War, at a time when military production was sharply increasing and the supply of labor sharply decreasing. Women were needed on the job to carry on the war effort, and many of them left their homes to work at jobs that women had never worked at before.

Other large-scale movements of women into the labor force occurred during the first and second World Wars, and to a lesser extent during the Korean and Vietnam wars. Usually their participation declined sharply in the postwar periods. Similarly, during periods of full employment, which often coincide with wars, their labor force participation has risen, and during recessions and depressions it has declined.

In effect, women have been a reserve work force (or at least part of a dual work force) called into action, like the military reserves, during periods of national need and retired from service once the emergency was over. In general, as their labor force participation has grown, so have their educational opportunities.

Not all women workers are part of this fluctuating reserve labor force. A rising proportion of them have become highly placed in the labor force and fully committed to it. Hence, their response to economic cycles is no greater than that of their male counterparts.

In recent decades the numbers of these fully committed women has been increased by rising educational levels, the tenure of women in their jobs, the growing need among women for financial independence, and the increasing awareness among women that they have a full commitment to work.

During periods of economic recession, women have usually been laid off their jobs arbitrarily and out of line with their seniority. The justification given by employers has been that, if they are married, their husbands can support them. More recently, the job rights of women have been protected to some extent by tenure and seniority rules written into union contracts or professional agreements. In the long run, the enforcement of these rights can reduce the sensitivity of women workers to fluctuations in the labor market. But in the short run, women are still more susceptible to layoffs than men are, simply because they tend to have less seniority on the job.

Equal rights legislation has also intervened to reduce the discrimination that keeps the market from being a truly free one. Such intervention of law and public policy in the market will have its maximum effect, however, in a full employment economy, when the demand for labor is high and the opportunities for women in the labor force are, therefore, also high. During periods of high unemployment, however, the effects of such intervention have not yet been tested. What remains to be settled is the strength of equal rights legislation during periods of declining need for women in the labor force.

Experience has shown that if women are needed in specific jobs, they will be trained and educated to fill those jobs. When they are not needed, they are retired to the reserves. The question for the future

Table 7.   Women in the Labor Force by Age and Years of School Completed, March, 1974

	25 to 34	35 to 44	45 to 54	55 and over
4 or more years of college	21%	13%	10%	10%
1 to 3 years of college	17%	12%	11%	11%
4 years of high school	44%	48%	48%	36%
1 to 3 years of high school	12%	17%	17%	17%
8 years of elementary school or less	4%	9%	14%	26%

Young women workers had more formal education than their older counterparts.

is: To what extent can the force of law, operating against sex discrimination in schools and on the job, keep women from being retired to the reserves when the market no longer requires their services?

Rescheduling and Redefinition of Work and School

Most young mothers have difficulty committing themselves fully to work, school, or other activities outside the home. Many take part-time jobs, but many more simply drop out of the labor force for a period of years while their children are young.

Unfortunately, most jobs are designed to suit male schedules in that they require long and regular working hours. The training and educational programs that prepare people for many jobs also tend to be designed without regard for the time schedules for young mothers.

At the highest vocational level, most graduate and professional programs, such as medical education, have demanded an extended and full-time commitment of students. Moreover, the commitment comes during the very years when women have a maximum commitment to young children.

Flexible and intermittent scheduling of both jobs and schooling will offer greater opportunities to women. They will then have greater freedom to schedule their school and working hours to suit their family obligations. Greater redefinition of the jobs themselves is also needed, along with the creation of new career lines to meet the time and scheduling needs of young mothers.

In this connection, more attention might be given to work and studies that women can do either entirely or mainly at home. In higher education, the university without walls concept, which grants credits for life experience and offers flexibly scheduled education, is particularly well suited to the needs of young mothers. The weekend college might also permit the

Table 8. Major Occupation Group of Employed Persons, by Sex, Race, and Years of School Completed: 1959 and 1971

[Relates to civilian noninstitutional population 18 years old and over as of March of years indicated. Based on Current Population Survey]

Year, Sex, and Occupation Group		White			Negro and Others		
		Total	Less than 4 years of high school	4 years of high school or more	Total	Less than 4 years of high school	4 years of high school or more
1959							
Male, number	1,000	37,766	18,740	19,026	3,745	2,928	816
Percent, by occupation:							
White collar		39.7	20.3	58.8	12.6	5.3	38.8
Blue collar		45.5	58.9	32.3	59.3	65.4	37.3
Service, incl. private household workers		5.6	7.2	4.0	14.3	12.6	20.2
Farm		9.2	13.7	4.9	13.9	16.7	3.7
Female, number	1,000	17,776	6,994	10,782	2,484	1,725	759

Percent, by occupation:						
White collar	61.1	31.5	80.8	17.6	5.8	44.5
Blue collar	17.2	31.4	8.0	14.7	15.7	12.4
Service, incl. private household workers	18.5	31.6	10.0	64.3	73.8	42.6
Farm	3.2	5.5	1.6	3.4	4.7	0.5
Male, number ... 1,000	42,159	13,737	28,422	4,575	2,503	2,072
Percent, by occupation:						
White collar	44.6	18.5	67.2	22.1	8.2	38.8
Blue collar	43.7	63.3	34.2	57.9	66.9	47.1
Service, incl. private household workers	7.0	9.7	5.7	15.2	17.3	12.7
Farm	4.8	8.5	3.0	4.8	7.7	1.3
Female, number ... 1,000	24,998	6,616	18,382	3,527	1,549	1,978
Percent, by occupation:						
White collar	64.9	29.9	77.4	37.8	11.6	58.3
Blue collar	15.3	34.4	8.4	17.2	20.7	14.4
Service, incl. private household workers	18.6	33.2	13.4	44.3	66.4	27.0
Farm	1.2	2.6	0.8	0.7	1.3	0.3

1971

Source: U.S. Bureau of Labor Statistics, *Special Labor Force Report*.

young mother to attend classes while her husband or others care for the children.

At the secondary level, examinations in lieu of class attendance, such as the General Education Diploma (for high school equivalency) will permit young mothers to continue their high school studies at home or during classes scheduled for hours when their husbands are home. The substitution of demonstrated skill and knowledge during all phases of the educational experience may significantly reduce the school penalties imposed on young mothers.

At the other end of the age continuum, among mature women whose children are grown and who are therefore freer to leave home for work and study, greater reentry opportunities are needed, both in schools and in the labor force. These mature women have become a significant part of the labor force. Many opportunities have opened to them, but employers are still reluctant to train older women for responsible jobs, and many educational programs have been reluctant to admit them as students.

Beyond the Market

While the strongest motivation for schooling is undoubtedly vocational, other motives are also present. It may even be that people tend to overvalue work-oriented education, just as they may tend to overvalue work itself. Those who *must* work cannot escape such a vocational orientation, of course, but those who have other options, as many women do, can turn to what may be more enriching learning experiences. In this connection it is useful to bear in mind that more than half of all women over age 18 are housewives rather than wage earners. Many of these housewives might prefer nonvocational types of education.

The function of education that would seem to have value greater than that contributed by paid work, from the point of view of general social benefits, is education that expands the community and political participation of women.

Such education, especially when carried into the neighborhoods where women live, can offer information and skills to housewives who wish to improve the quality of community life. Such learning is especially well suited to the needs of housewives and others who remain at home either out of necessity or preference, for it is simply a continuation of the kind of community work in which many are already engaged.

From the experience gained in community education, women would then be better able to involve themselves successfully in political life at local, state, and national levels. In this way they could exercise far greater influence in the society than women with full-time work commitments might be able to do. The subject will be dealt with somewhat more fully in the concluding chapter.

10

Vocational Education

Most education is vocational in the sense that people go to school mainly to qualify for better jobs. The motive is present even in general and liberal arts education since employers usually require certificates of general education competency (high school diplomas or college degrees) whether or not such education is related directly—or at all—to the jobs being performed.

Professional education is, of course, strictly vocational even though it is carried on in university classrooms rather than shops or labs. Higher education simply prepares people for higher level jobs, but the status of the job does not make the training any less vocational.

The term vocational education, however, applies more narrowly to training for jobs that could better be classified as skilled, semi-skilled, or technical, rather than professional or managerial. It generally applies, in effect, to occupations that do not require a college degree.

Vocational education encompasses a vast and scattered network of training, including programs conducted under public sponsorship, those offered by employers themselves, and those offered by private vocational schools. The chief difference in these sponsorships is the source of payment: government, employer, student—respectively.

Historic and Current

Vocational education first became a matter of serious public concern at the time of the Civil War when the historic Morrill Act was passed, providing states with federal land grants to enable them to carry on research and education in agriculture and mechanics (A & M). The schools and cooperative extension programs that were generated by this Act may have been the most successful in the history of education, giving rise as they did to a revolution in American agriculture—to the neglect of the mechanics half of their mission. Most of the services and education provided to women in these programs have been in home economics.

Public vocational programs in primary and secondary schools came into being around the turn of the century. They were a response to early demands to make schools more relevant to the real world, as well as to employer demands that students be taught skills and behavior that would make them more productive workers.

Manual training was viewed in the early days as a way not only of vitalizing the classroom but of teaching students the value of artisanship (a vanishing attribute) and industriousness. The early manual training was in a sense a moral movement, aimed at rescuing the artisan from the alienating influence of industry and the division of labor. The movement was soon transformed, however, into an effort by employers to prepare students for industrial work.

In 1917 the Smith-Hughes Act was passed and the federal government for the first time entered the business of vocational education. Before that, either employers had to pay for their own training programs, or training was conducted by journeymen or master craftsmen through the apprenticeship system.

The immediate incentive for the passage of the Smith-Hughes Act was World War I and the production needs of a war economy. Employers argued that Germany had risen to a position of industrial power at least in part because of publicly supported vocational educational programs. They insisted that winning the war and competing in world markets necessitated federal intervention in vocational training. Employers were also eager to prevent unions from dominating trade and apprenticeship training, as they had come to do. For its part, organized labor opposed business domination of any publicly funded vocational programs, and sought and won representation on all the policy boards of these programs.

In 1913 Edwin G. Cooley, a former Chicago school superintendent, had offered a bill to the legislature to divide the state's schools into separate vocational and general schools starting with grade 7. The bill was sponsored by the business community. John Dewey insisted that such separations would lead to even greater divisions between the working and the leisured classes, and with the active support of organized labor, the bill was defeated. The comprehensive school won out in Illinois and most other places, but it still contained within it vocational and ability groups that separated working class students from others and working class males from their female counterparts.

Other vocational acts followed Smith-Hughes, but not until the Vocational Education Act of 1963 and its amendments in 1968 did any major changes in federal support for vocational education develop. The amendments of 1968 stressed the needs of disadvantaged and handicapped youth and adults, as well as the need to expand technical programs at the postsecondary level.

Legislation has also expanded work experience programs—i.e., work-study and cooperative education. The work-study programs provide part-time paid jobs for needy vocational education students. They are designed to permit these young students to stay in high school. Cooperative education, a program that

Table 9. Women Enrolled in Public

Program	All women enrollees			Secondary school courses	
	Number	Percent distri-bution	As percent of total enrollees	Number	Percent distri-bution
Total	3,827,166	100.0	54.3	2,349,070	100.0
Home economics[1]	2,101,221	54.9	96.2	1,416,185	60.3
Job-oriented courses	57,025	1.5	91.6	18,286	.8
Office occupations	1,214,925	31.7	77.3	781,459	33.3
Distribution	214,314	5.6	44.6	74,446	3.2
Trades and industry	155,808	4.1	10.5	53,849	2.3
Health occupations	109,005	2.8	94.7	15,773	.7
Technical education	22,890	.6	8.6	2,445	.1
Agriculture	9,003	.2	1.0	4,913	.2

[1] Includes women in courses not shown separately.

Source: U.S. Department of Health, Education, and Welfare, Office of Education, Division of Vocational and Technical Education.

has long been a feature of trade, industrial, and distributive (business) education, is more a training than an aid program. It allows students to alternate periods of work and study. The work provides on-the-job experience which is linked to course work and is subject to public supervision.

Enrollments of women in vocational courses have increased more rapidly than enrollments of men. By the end of the sixties, about 4 million women were enrolled in public vocational education courses. About 6 percent of these were in postsecondary schools, about 32 percent in adult extension courses, and approximately 61 percent in secondary schools.

In 1962 about 11.6 million people were enrolled in vocational education programs—7 million in secondary schools, 1.3 million in postsecondary schools (mainly community colleges), and 2.9 million in adult education. Most public vocational programs are now located in vocational high schools or in two-year community colleges. In many cases the level and quality of these vocational schools has been significantly upgraded.

Vocational Courses, by Type of Program, 1966-67

Postsecondary-school courses		Adult extension courses		Special needs programs	
Number	Percent distribution	Number	Percent distribution	Number	Percent distribution
214,617	100.0	1,228,159	100.0	35,320	100.0
3,036	1.4	659,501	53.7	22,499	63.7
2,744	1.3	31,762	2.6	4,236	12.0
128,509	59.9	301,494	24.5	3,463	9.8
6,698	3.1	130,917	10.7	2,253	6.4
17,189	8.0	79,218	6.5	5,552	15.7
51,008	23.8	40,837	3.3	1,387	3.9
7,509	3.5	12,881	1.0	55	.2
668	.3	3,311	.3	111	.3

Vocational education in public schools has been criticized over the years for its class and sex segregation of students and for its irrelevancy to changing demands of the labor market and of specific jobs. Vast and increasing sums of public money are being invested in these public programs. The total amount spent in 1972 was $2.7 billion—up from $239 million in 1960. About a fifth of this money comes from the federal government, the rest from state and local governments.

Sex Segregation

Fifty-five percent of enrollees in 1972 in public vocational education programs were female. These female students were concentrated in a few sex-stereotyped vocational areas. More than half were in home economics or consumer programs. About three-fourths were either in homemaking or in office skills programs. On the other hand, better than 58 percent of males were enrolled in technical, industrial, agricultural programs. About half of all the course categories had more than 90 percent enrollment of one or the other

sex, and 71 percent of the categories had enrollments
of 75 percent of one or the other sex.

Females in vocational programs tend to be more
highly concentrated in a few occupations than male
students are, and the occupations in which they are
concentrated also tend to pay less and offer fewer
benefits than occupations for which males study.
Figures reported by states show that seven times more
males than females were enrolled in industrial and
trade programs in 1972. More than 37,000 men were
being trained as plumbers, for example, but only
thirty-four women. Men outnumbered women in business data processing and management, and they were
more than seven times more numerous in automotive
courses, twenty times more numerous in petroleum
courses. Women were three times more numerous than
men in clerical courses and twice as numerous as men
in apparel courses.

Many vocational schools have been sex exclusive.
In New York City for example, only eight of the
twenty-seven vocational high schools were coeducational in 1970. Six schools were for girls only and
thirteen for boys, including schools in printing, food,
maritime studies, aviation, automotive trades. The boys
schools enrolled more than twice as many students
as the girls schools (7,600 girls and 19,800 boys). Girls
had a choice of thirty-six courses while the boys could
choose from more than twice that number. Moreover,
the boys were generally enrolled in courses that led
to greater opportunity and chances for advancement
than did the female courses. Even within some coeducational schools, the sexes were put into separate
classes, as in the High School of Fashion Industries,
where different courses or sections were offered to
males and females.

After girls challenged in the courts their exclusion
from two all-male prestige high schools in New York
City (Stuyvesant and the Bronx High School of
Science), open enrollment in all high schools in the

city, including academic and vocational, became official policy.

Like graduate and professional education, vocational education is more sex discriminatory than are the various forms of general and liberal arts education. Early in the century, vocational education for women involved mainly cooking and sewing, skills that women could use as homemakers but also as dressmakers, milliners, cooks, housekeepers. Beginning sometime after World War I, vocational education for women has concentrated also on office skills, but since then little change has taken place in the programs available.

The commonest rationalizations for the exclusion of women from traditional male programs have been that women cannot get jobs in the trade or vocation so it is useless to train them and that qualified applicants cannot be found. Women cannot get jobs in male vocations, however, until they have the training, and until they get training and jobs, there are unlikely to be many qualified applicants.

Barriers

Barriers to progress for women in vocational education are found not only among employers and employees who control the jobs, but also among those who control vocational education itself. Males are overwhelmingly dominant in the vocational education policy boards and the control of traditional male jobs.

The Federal Vocational Education Act of 1963, as amended in 1968, requires, for example, that the states must establish two groups: a State Vocational Education Board and a State Advisory Commission. Of the 1,168 members of these key policy groups throughout the nation, only 159—or 14 percent of the total—were women in one recent year. Six states had no women at all on their advisory councils and another nineteen states had only one or two women. Males also dominate policy-making levels in the U.S. Department of Health,

Education, and Welfare, where the vocational education acts are administered and where the equal opportunities laws in education are enforced.

Furthermore, stereotyped attitudes about women in traditional male trades have been reported among instructors in trade courses, recruiters who interview junior high school students, and in the recruitment literature for vocational programs.

Remedies

Title IX of the Education Amendments of 1972 stipulates that no person shall, on the basis of sex, be subjected to discrimination under any education program or activity receiving federal financial assistance. (See Chapter 13)

All vocational education programs and schools, private or public, are covered by the amendment, as are all faculty and administration, students, and applicants of those programs. The amendment required that all federally funded vocational schools must immediately admit students without regard to sex. Programs that were completely sex segregated as of June, 1972 or before June, 1965 were given one year to comply with general admission requirements and about seven years to comply with all requirements. In these cases, a schedule for eliminating discrimination was required, along with a plan for a recruitment program to encourage enrollment of the excluded sex.

All vocational and career education programs that receive federal funds are under the Bureau of Occupational and Adult Education of the U.S. Office of Education, Department of Health, Education, and Welfare. Applicants for funds from that bureau must pledge that funds will not be used in programs that discriminate. It has been noted, however, that the procedures for reviewing compliance have been quite inadequate and that enforcement has suffered from an insufficiency of commitment on the part of the enforcement agents.

Table 10

HEW has projected enrollment to 1977 and predicts virtually no change in the percentage distribution of enrollment by sex over the next four years, as shown here:

	1972	1977 (projected)
Agriculture		
Male	94.6	92.0
Female	5.4	8.0
Distribution		
Male	54.7	54.0
Female	45.3	46.0
Health		
Male	15.3	17.0
Female	84.7	83.0
Home Economics		
Male	8.4	10.0
Female	91.6	90.0
Office		
Male	23.6	25.0
Female	76.4	75.0
Technical		
Male	90.2	91.0
Female	9.8	9.0
Trade and Industry		
Male	88.3	87.0
Female	11.7	13.0

Center for Adult, Vocational, Technical, and Manpower Education, Division of Vocational and Technical Education, Office of Education, U.S. Dep't of HEW, Trends in Vocational Education, Fiscal Year 1972, June, 1973, at 7. As the above figures indicate, HEW apparently does not foresee Title IX as having any impact on vocational education.

Policy

Among the proposals offered to reduce sex discrimination in vocational education are that federal agencies identify the vocational needs of women as well as the special vocational opportunities open to them, and that model training programs be created, along with new career guidance materials and approaches. It is proposed that all vocational programs be examined for sex bias at local, state, and federal levels, that all government boards and agencies dealing with vocational education be examined with a view to improving the representation of women on them, and that training programs be launched to familiarize all personnel with regulations governing sex discrimination, and with the research, new materials, and curricula on vocational education for women.

11

Job and "Manpower" Training

Historically jobs have been so closely associated with male activities that when, during the sixties, the federal government began to fund programs specifically aimed at job preparation, usually at low skill levels, those programs became known as manpower training programs. The name, widely applied, has not yet been changed to include the female of the species, although some of them have come to be called human resource development programs, and all of them enroll large numbers of women.

Manpower programs—and also antipoverty programs—initiated in the sixties during a period of relatively full employment, had several objectives, all aimed at reducing poverty and discrimination: to help disadvantaged people find employment, to help employers find qualified workers, and to help upgrade impoverished communities. These programs proliferated into what became, in many cases, a stunning array of innovative experiments in education and training. The most innovative, of course, were those aimed at community organization. Such efforts had never before been attempted by government or subsidized by public funds.

The first major law enacted was the federal Manpower Development and Training Act of 1962 (MDTA), which authorized the promotion and funding of job training programs for the unemployed and underemployed. The Department of Labor handled

Table 11. Manpower Programs: Number and Percent by Selected Characteristics of Enrollees in Major Programs; Summary, Fiscal Years 1965-1972
(Numbers in thousands)

Program	All Enrollees Total[a]	Sex — Women		Age Under 22 Years		Education Less Than 12 Years		Received Public Assistance	
		Total	Percent	Total	Percent	Total	Percent	Total	Percent
MDTA									
Institutional	1,184	530	44.8	494	41.7	668	56.4	162	13.7
OJT	626	190	30.4	221	35.3	299	47.8	32	5.1
Neighborhood Youth Corps									
In-school[b]	4,070	1,840	45.2	4,070	100.0	3,966	97.4	1,318	32.4
Out-of-school[b]	917	437	47.7	903	98.5	800	87.2	272	29.7
Concentrated Employment Program	469	199	42.4	193	41.2	307	65.5	64	13.6
Work Incentive Program	406	256	63.1	98	24.1	261	64.3	403	99.3
Job Opportunities in the Business Sector	313	99	31.6	144	46.0	195	62.3	48	15.3
Job Corps[c]	233	63	27.0	233	100.0	213	91.4	79	33.9
Public Employment Program	305	85	27.9	70	23.0	82	26.9	37	12.1
Public Service Careers[d]	112	72	64.3	23	20.5	40	35.7	22	19.6
Opportunities Industrialization Centers	163	114	69.9	54	33.1	122	74.8	102	62.6
Apprenticeship Outreach Program	22	n.a.	n.a.	20	90.9	2	9.1	n.a.	n.a.
Operation Mainstream[a]	90	23	25.6	3	3.3	69	76.7	18	20.0
Total	8,910	3,908	43.9	6,526	73.2	7,024	78.8	2,557	28.7

The Impact of Government Manpower Programs, C.R. Perry, et al., The Wharton School, U. of Pa., 1975, p. 22.
[a]Includes MDTA Institutional and OJT programs
[b]Includes JOBS, PSC, PEP, and AOP programs
[c]Includes OIC, CEP, WIN, and Job Corps programs
[d]Includes NYC-In-School, Summer, and Out-of-School programs
Note: Percents may not add to 100.0 due to rounding

the job-related aspects of training, and HEW the general education components.

The Economic Opportunities Act of 1964 then created the Office of Economic Opportunities (OEO) for the purpose of promoting and funding a variety of antipoverty training and community based programs. These offered a range of services, training, and education for the poor, aimed largely at stimulating self-help and socially useful employment.

After less than a decade, the OEO, under a new national administration, was dismantled, and both its functions and those of the MDTA were largely superseded by the Comprehensive Employment and Training Act (CETA) of 1973. The main thrust of CETA was to turn over responsibility for developing programs from the federal to the state and local governments. The so-called categorical programs and state and local governments were no longer required to create and fund programs in specified categories. Only the Job Corps and WIN (Work Incentives for welfare recipients) remained under the administration of the federal government.

Between 1965 and 1972, about nine million people had enrolled in the major manpower programs supported by federal funds. Blacks were about 46 percent of the total and women about 43 percent. About seven in ten participants were under 22 years of age, and about three in four had less than a high school diploma.

Women were well represented in many of the programs and they were a majority in WIN, Public Service Careers (often in the health occupations), and Opportunities Industrialization Centers, but they were under-represented in some of the large and more costly programs, such as the Job Corps. No determination has yet been made of the relative costs and benefits to women of these manpower programs. Such an inquiry would be extremely difficult, since the programs are so varied in their costs per trainee and in

Table 12. Manpower Programs: Percent Distribution of
Enrollment Among Major Program Groups

Program Group	Nonminority	Blacks	Female
Skill Training[a]	27.2	15.5	18.4
Job Development[b]	8.4	8.3	6.5
Employability Development[c]	11.7	18.3	16.2
Work Experience[d]	54.5	57.4	58.3
Total	100.0	100.0	100.0

The Impact of Government Manpower Programs, C.R. Perry et al., The Wharton School,
U. of Pa., 1975, p. 24.
Source: Derived from Table 2.
[a] Includes MDTA Institutional and OJT programs
[b] Includes JOBS, PSC, PEP, and AOP programs
[c] Includes OIC, CEP, WIN, and Job Corps programs
[d] Includes NYC-In-School, Summer, and Out-of-School programs
Note: Percents may not add to 100.0 due to rounding.

their impact on trainees. An important step in that
direction was taken, however, in a study conducted
at The Wharton School, *The Impact of Government
Manpower Programs, in General, and on Minorities
and Women.*

Among female participants in manpower programs,
a majority participated in work experience programs
rather than in the training and education programs.
This was also true for male participation, but less
so. Women were less likely than males to receive skill
training and more likely to participate in employability
development programs (including general education)
than were males.

MDTA

By the mid-sixties, training under the Manpower
Development and Training Act (MDTA), the largest
of the training efforts, had become an important part
of the war on poverty, directing about two-thirds of
its training efforts to the disadvantaged and about
a third to training in skills that were in short supply.

In an analysis of the institutional programs of MDTA
it was found that about 50 percent of women enrollees

were family heads, about 40 percent had three or more dependents, and 17 percent received public assistance. About half were school dropouts. Women of all ages were enrolled.

Women were less likely than males to participate

Table 13. Percentage of Women Enrolled in MDTA Programs, by Selected Occupations, Fiscal Year 1968

Occupation	Type of training	
	Institutional	On-the-job
Number	62,000	40,000
Percent	100	100
Professional, technical, and managerial[1]	27	4
Professional nurse (refresher)	9	—
Occupations in medicine and health[2]	15	—
Clerical and sales[1]	41	15
Computing and account recording (n.e.c.)	9	4
Stenographer	9	—
Stenographer-typist and related	14	—
Service[1]	23	32
Attendants, home and first aid	—	19
Attendants, hospital and related[3]	13	—
Chefs and cooks (large hotels and restaurants)	3	—
Waitress and related	—	4
Farming, fishing, forestry	(4)	(4)
Processing[1]	(4)	6
Mixing and blending (chemicals, plastics, etc.)	—	3
Machine trades	2	12
Bench work[1]	5	22
Electronic components assembly and repair.	—	4
Structural work	2	7
All other occupations	(4)	2

[1] Includes women being trained in occupations not shown separately.

[2] Includes licensed practical nurse, surgical technician, inhalation therapist, medical laboratory technician, and dentist's assistant.

[3] Includes nurses' aide, ward attendant, psychiatric aide, and tray-line worker.

[4] Less than 1 percent.

Source: U.S. Department of Labor, Manpower Administration.

Table 14.   Economic Impact of Manpower Programs: MDTA Median Hourly Wage Rates of Trainees Pre- and Post-Training by Sex and Race

Years	Institutional			On-the-Job		
	Pre-	Post-	Gains	Pre-	Post-	Gains
1967–1968						
Total	$1.55	$2.04	$0.49	$1.74	$2.29	$0.55
Male	1.79	2.31	.52	1.97	2.63	.66
Female	1.40	1.81	.41	1.54	1.88	.34
1970–1971						
Total	1.93	2.23	.30	2.13	2.44	.31
Male	2.17	2.49	.32	2.37	2.71	.34
Female	1.77	2.10	.33	1.81	2.01	.20
White	1.96	2.27	.31	2.18	2.53	.35
Black	1.87	2.17	.30	1.96	2.23	.27
1971–1972						
Total	2.07	2.25	.18	2.52	2.68	.16
Male	2.40	2.68	.28	3.05	3.21	.16
Female	1.82	1.97	.15	1.87	2.15	.28
White	2.15	2.37	.22	2.72	2.90	.18
Black	1.90	2.11	.21	2.15	2.36	.21

The Impact of Government Manpower Programs, C.R. Perry et al., The Wharton School, U. of Pa., 1975, p. 52.

Sources: "The Influence of MDTA Training on Earnings," Manpower Evaluation Report No. 8. Manpower Administration, U.S. Department of Labor, 1970.

"Earnings Mobility of MDTA Graduates." Manpower Evaluation Report No. 7, Manpower Administration, U.S. Department of Labor, 1969.

U.S. Department of Labor, "Median Earnings of Terminees From the MDTA Institutional and OJT Programs in FY 1971 and FY 1972," unpublished Manpower Administration report, 1972.

in the on-the-job programs of MDTA because employers were less likely to select them for training. When they did participate in on-the-job training, their hourly rates of pay were likely to be higher and the pay gains they made through training were also likely to be higher than gains derived from institutional training. In both institutional and on-the-job training, their pay rates were lower than those of males.

The women participants in MDTA were mainly in training for traditional female occupations in health and in office work, but a rather significant number were trained in traditionally male occupations.

These job training programs were all new and innovative efforts. They were designed essentially to reach people who were unemployed or underemployed mainly because they had not benefited much from formal schooling and had not acquired useful job skills there or elsewhere. Many of these disadvantaged people were, of course, unemployed less because they lacked skills or education than because jobs were not available, or because the available jobs offered so little in pay or demanded so much in labor that applicants were not attracted to them.

The programs sought to match people with available jobs, but some also sought to deal with the shortage of decent jobs by developing and creating new jobs, mainly in the public sector but also in the private. These jobs were usually better paying or more socially and personally meaningful than available jobs.

At their best, these programs did what the public schools and vocational education programs within the schools were often less able or unable to do. They reached the disadvantaged and taught them job and learning skills in preparation for, or in conjunction with, employment in specific jobs. In doing so they often bridged the chasm that separates school and society.

Moreover, because the programs were more closely linked to the job market than to general education, they went beyond training and education. They sought to affect and to some extent restructure and upgrade the job market itself, creating new and relatively rewarding jobs, and launching efforts to employ people in community improvement.

The approach merits a closer examination than can be given here. Its implications for women lie in the special attention given to upgrading the employability of women and finding a place in the labor force for them as well as in the creation of career lines, the restructuring of work, and the launching of community improvement efforts.

Apprenticeship Training

The job training programs hitherto referred to were all new and innovative efforts, designed mainly to reach economically and educationally disadvantaged groups. As we have seen, these programs were, in the aggregate, directed almost as much at women as at men. While women are somewhat less than 50 percent of the labor force, they were about 43 percent of all trainees in these programs.

Apprenticeship training is almost the opposite, in many ways, of these manpower programs. It is directed less at the disadvantaged than at white working class groups, and it includes relatively few women trainees. As the demand for greater job opportunities for minorities, women, and the poor have grown, apprenticeship programs, like most other vocational training programs, have turned attention, however reluctantly in some cases, to the inclusion of minorities among their trainees.

Apprenticeship training is probably the oldest and most venerable type of trade training, dating back in its structured form at least to the medieval period in Western history, when young men (and sometimes young women) apprenticed themselves as learners and assistants to a journeyman or master craftsman. After a period of years, the apprentice became a journeyman craftsman himself and set up his own shop.

Now apprenticeship training is part of a vast network of training and education programs carried on mainly outside public schools and supervised by the Bureau of Apprenticeship and Training of the U.S. Department of Labor. The Bureau operates field offices which approve training standards and promote programs for some 370 skilled trades.

Apprenticeship is on-the-job training, just as internship is for doctors. Usually training programs run about four years and are operated jointly by employers and labor unions to train people for specific existing job openings. The trades taught are usually in choice occupations that pay relatively well and are relatively secure.

Less than 1 percent of the more than 300,000 apprentices currently in training are women, although women have worked at most trades and demonstrated their competence in many of them, especially during the two World Wars.

By the end of the sixties, women were being trained in forty-seven different apprenticeship programs, including programs for bookbinders, dental technicians, cosmetologists, dressmakers—as well as some non-traditional trades such as plumber, machinist, and clock repairer. Many of these trades represent the most traditional of male occupations. The common assumption is that, because they are so traditionally male, they will be among the most difficult of occupations for women to enter, and among those women will be least interested in entering. Experience indicates that the barriers to the entry of women are less formidable than is often assumed. These trades, and the apprenticeship programs that prepare for them, are of special importance to women not only because they offer rewarding employment but also because they are an important part of the male dominated technical-mechanical structure of the whole society. Barred from knowledge of their mysteries, women may continue to play only marginal roles in what is a basically technological society.

Private Programs

Beyond these publicly sponsored or supervised programs is another vast assortment of job training programs conducted by employers and by privately operated schools. These programs offer a range of training, from the minimal to the most advanced skills. Few efforts have been made to examine the impact of these programs on women or the role that women play in them.

The census of each decade from 1900 to 1960 has shown women to be only 2 or 3 percent of all skilled workers. During World War II, women were 5 percent of skilled workers, a significant gain over previous years but still a small part of the total. After the war, the proportion declined, but during the sixties some strides were again made. Among women in the skilled trades, the increase rate of about 80 percent was twice as great as in any other occupation, and eight times as great as the rate for men. By 1970, women held as large a proportion of the skilled jobs as they had held during World War II. Gains were made in a variety of nontraditional trades.

In fourteen trades the number of women increased by 5,000 or more, only two of the trades being traditional occupations for women (baker and decorator). Two of the occupations were supervisory. The other ten were nontraditional: auto mechanic, carpenter, compositor and typesetter, dental laboratory technician, electrician, heavy equipment mechanic, machinist, painter, printing press operator, and telephone installer and repairer.

What is remarkable about this growth is that the trades grew very little during the sixties, while clerical and professional occupations, traditional occupations for women, grew rapidly. Still, the participation of women increased more rapidly in the trades than in these fast growing occupations.

Women in the skilled trades tend to be much like other women except that they are older, less educated, and more often from blue-collar families. Two in five were high school graduates in 1970, and about one in ten had a year or more of college. They were more likely than other women workers to be widows or divorcees and less likely to be single. About nine in ten were white, as were women in the total labor force. About a quarter of the married women had husbands who were skilled workers, and about a quarter had husbands who were less skilled blue-collar workers.

During the sixties, their average schooling rose one year, three times the rise for other women workers.

Enrollments of women in public school trade and industrial programs, many of them pre-apprenticeship, increased from 116,000 in 1966 to 280,000 in 1972, a rate of increase half again greater than that of men.

The Bureau of Apprenticeship and Training requires that all trades apply nondiscriminatory standards in the recruitment, selection, and employment of apprentices. Women have some advantage in entry to apprenticeship programs because entry is usually based in part on written tests in which women tend to perform well.

On the General Aptitude Test Battery, used to relate aptitudes to job requirements, seven areas are regarded as important to success in the trades. Among these women excel in four (form perception, clerical perception, motor coordination, finger dexterity), men in one (spatial reasoning), and males and females are the same on two (numerical reasoning, manual dexterity).

Levels of physical strength required on various skilled jobs have been determined by the U.S. Department of Labor. Data are not available on the relative levels of strength of males and females, but many trades require no more physical strength than is required for housekeeping, while other trades require strength even beyond the ability of many men (but within the ability of *some* women).

Apprenticeship training offers students much more than most types of job training: paid jobs, two to four years of on-the-job training and classroom instruction, sick leave, paid vacations, coverage by workmen's compensation, and other fringe benefits.

12

Academic Women

More has been written about academic women than about any other group of women, perhaps because they do so much of the research and writing about women.

In higher education, women constitute between a fifth and a quarter of teaching and professional staff. They are over-represented in the faculties of small colleges and community colleges, where they are 40 percent of faculty, and under-represented in the major universities and high prestige colleges.

They tend to be in the lower professional levels at the universities and either not on the tenure track or in the lower ranks of that track. Males are twice as likely to be tenured as women (57 and 28 percent, respectively).

Nationally, women are 32 percent of instructors, 19 percent of assistant professors, 15 percent of associate professors, and only 8 percent of full professors. Even at the seven women's "Ivy League" colleges, women are 82 percent of the nonprofessional teaching staff, 64 percent of the assistant professors, 54 percent of the associate professors, and 22 percent of the full professors. Furthermore, between 1965 and 1970, men replaced women as presidents of three of these seven colleges.

The slight decline since 1930 in women faculty as a proportion of total faculty may be attributed to the relative decline of females in education faculties and to the rapid increase in scientific, technological, and

Table 15. Professional Background and Academic Activity of College Faculty Members, by Type of Institution and by Sex: United States, 1972-73
[Percentage Distribution]

1	All Institutions			Universities			Four-Year Colleges			Two-Year Colleges		
	Total	Men	Women	Total	Men	Women	Total	Men	Women	Total	Men	Women
	2	3	4	5	6	7	8	9	10	11	12	13
Total	100.0	100.0	100.0	100.0	100.0	100.0	100.0	100.0	100.0	100.0	100.0	100.0
Highest degree currently held												
None, less than B.A. . . .	1.3	1.3	1.0	1.0	1.1	0.4	0.6	0.5	0.7	3.3	3.6	2.3
Bachelor's	4.9	4.5	6.5	5.1	4.9	6.3	3.2	2.8	4.3	8.2	7.3	10.9
Master's	44.9	40.8	61.6	30.8	25.0	59.9	47.0	44.3	56.3	73.5	73.6	73.2
LL.B., J.D., other professional (except medical)	5.0	5.4	3.7	6.1	6.6	3.8	4.7	5.1	3.6	3.1	2.9	3.8
Doctorate (except medical, Ed.D., or Ph.D.)	1.5	1.6	1.2	1.6	1.7	1.0	1.8	1.8	1.6	1.0	1.1	0.9
Ed.D.	3.0	3.1	2.6	2.7	2.7	2.7	3.8	4.0	3.1	1.6	1.7	1.4
Medical (M.D. or D.D.S.) . .	1.1	1.2	0.5	2.3	2.5	1.1	0.1	0.1	0.1	0.3	0.3	0.2
Ph.D.	30.2	33.8	15.6	40.2	44.9	16.4	31.4	34.2	21.5	4.3	4.5	3.4
(No answer)	8.1	8.3	7.4	10.3	10.6	8.5	7.3	7.1	8.2	4.7	4.9	4.0
Year highest degree received												
Before 1940	4.4	4.6	3.4	6.0	6.3	4.7	3.5	3.7	2.9	2.4	2.4	2.2
1940-1949	9.0	9.4	7.4	11.6	11.8	10.6	7.6	8.0	6.5	5.7	6.2	4.1
1950-1959	24.3	25.5	19.1	26.2	27.7	18.7	22.7	23.5	20.0	22.9	24.4	18.1
1960-1969	46.5	45.4	50.7	43.6	42.4	49.8	48.5	47.8	50.8	48.9	47.9	51.9

1970-present	10.5	9.8	12.9	8.5	7.8	11.6	12.5	12.1	13.8	10.9	10.1	13.5
No higher degree or no answer	5.5	5.2	6.5	4.1	4.0	4.7	5.1	4.9	6.0	9.2	8.9	10.2
Major field of highest degree												
Business	4.1	4.7	1.9	3.2	3.7	0.9	4.7	5.5	2.0	5.0	5.5	3.5
Education (including physical and health education)	14.8	12.6	23.4	11.3	9.1	21.9	16.3	13.9	24.8	19.8	18.8	22.9
Biological sciences (including agriculture)	6.8	7.4	4.3	9.2	10.1	4.7	4.9	5.1	4.2	5.1	5.4	4.1
Physical sciences (including mathematics/statistics, and computer sciences)	11.5	13.3	4.3	10.8	12.3	3.0	12.4	14.6	4.4	11.4	13.0	6.2
Engineering (including architecture/design)	6.3	7.8	0.4	8.9	10.5	0.8	4.6	5.8	0.3	4.0	5.3	0.0
Social sciences (including psychology and geography)	12.4	13.3	8.6	13.1	14.2	7.4	13.0	14.1	8.7	9.5	9.2	10.5
Fine arts	8.4	8.3	9.2	7.2	7.0	8.4	10.2	9.8	11.6	7.7	8.2	5.9
Humanities	17.6	16.8	20.6	14.3	14.0	15.7	21.2	20.5	23.9	17.7	16.2	22.3
Health sciences	4.6	3.2	10.2	8.2	6.6	16.4	1.5	0.5	5.1	3.0	0.6	10.1
Other professions (including social work, law, journalism, library science)	4.0	3.7	4.9	5.3	5.1	6.2	3.7	3.3	5.1	1.4	1.0	2.6
All other fields (including home economics, industrial arts, vocational-technical)	2.7	2.1	5.4	2.8	1.7	8.4	2.0	1.5	3.6	4.2	4.3	3.8

NOTE.—Data are based upon a sample survey. Because of rounding, percents may not add to 100.0.
SOURCE: American Council on Education, Research Report Vol. 8, No. 2, *Teaching Faculty in Academe: 1972-73.*

Table 15.—Continued

	All Institutions			Universities			Four-Year Colleges			Two-Year Colleges		
	Total	Men	Women	Total	Men	Women	Total	Men	Women	Total	Men	Women
1	2	3	4	5	6	7	8	9	10	11	12	13
None, no higher degree (including no answer)	6.7	6.7	6.6	5.8	5.7	6.2	5.5	5.3	6.3	11.4	12.5	8.1
Principal activity of current position:												
Administration	11.4	12.2	8.5	12.8	13.7	8.6	12.0	12.5	10.0	6.9	7.5	5.2
Teaching	82.2	81.2	86.5	75.8	74.2	83.5	85.4	84.9	87.2	90.6	90.8	89.8
Research	4.2	4.8	1.6	8.5	9.5	3.7	1.3	1.5	0.6	0.3	0.2	0.4
Other	2.2	1.9	3.4	2.9	2.6	4.2	1.4	1.1	2.2	2.2	1.5	4.6
Employment status for current academic year												
Full time	95.3	96.1	91.8	93.9	94.8	89.2	95.4	96.5	91.4	98.2	98.8	96.3
Part time, more than half time	1.3	0.9	2.9	1.6	1.2	3.8	1.4	0.9	3.2	0.5	0.3	1.2
Half time	1.2	0.8	2.7	1.3	0.9	3.5	1.4	1.0	2.9	0.6	0.4	1.2
Less than half time	2.2	2.1	2.6	3.2	3.1	3.5	1.9	1.7	2.5	0.7	0.6	1.3
Present rank:												
Professor	26.4	30.3	11.0	36.2	40.9	12.3	24.3	27.8	11.9	8.0	8.2	7.4
Associate professor	24.3	25.1	21.0	25.4	26.4	20.4	27.2	27.8	24.9	15.5	15.8	14.6
Assistant professor	25.3	23.8	31.2	24.4	22.3	35.1	32.2	30.8	37.1	12.9	12.5	13.9
Instructor	13.2	10.4	24.3	8.7	5.9	22.8	10.8	8.6	18.4	29.0	26.2	37.8
Lecturer	2.5	2.2	4.0	3.2	2.7	5.8	2.8	2.4	4.3	0.4	0.4	0.4
Do not hold rank designation	6.7	6.8	6.4	0.5	0.5	0.4	1.6	1.6	1.6	32.1	34.4	25.0
Other rank	1.6	1.4	2.1	1.7	1.4	3.2	1.1	1.0	1.8	2.1	2.5	1.0

Number of hours per week in scheduled teaching:												
None, or no answer	6.6	6.4	7.6	7.2	7.1	7.9	6.2	5.9	7.1	6.4	5.8	8.0
One to four hours	11.8	12.5	9.0	17.8	18.8	12.9	9.0	9.2	8.6	3.7	3.7	3.5
Five to eight hours	21.8	23.2	16.2	32.6	34.6	22.5	17.5	18.0	15.8	5.9	5.5	7.2
Nine to twelve hours	28.3	28.3	28.1	25.2	24.5	28.7	39.6	40.5	36.6	11.4	11.5	11.1
Thirteen to sixteen hours	17.3	16.2	21.9	8.8	7.7	14.3	17.5	17.2	18.8	36.7	35.7	40.0
Seventeen hours or more	14.1	13.3	17.1	8.4	7.3	13.6	10.1	9.3	13.1	35.9	37.7	30.2
Current base institutional salary:												
$6,500 or less	2.7	2.0	5.7	2.9	2.3	6.1	2.9	2.1	6.3	1.7	0.9	4.1
$6,600–$9,500	7.0	4.4	17.6	4.3	2.2	14.7	9.2	6.0	21.5	8.7	6.6	15.5
$9,600–$11,500	12.5	10.4	21.4	9.0	6.4	22.0	16.9	15.3	22.8	11.6	9.6	18.0
$11,600–$13,500	16.4	16.2	17.3	13.9	12.8	19.1	19.4	20.4	15.7	15.9	15.5	17.2
$13,600–$15,500	15.8	16.5	13.1	15.0	15.1	14.6	15.1	16.3	10.6	19.1	20.4	15.0
$15,600–$17,500	13.2	14.2	8.9	12.6	13.2	9.4	10.4	11.5	6.0	20.5	22.7	13.3
$17,600–$19,500	9.9	10.9	5.5	10.6	11.8	4.5	7.3	8.0	4.7	13.4	15.0	8.4
$19,600–$21,500	6.8	7.7	2.8	8.8	9.9	3.4	6.0	6.9	2.6	3.7	4.2	2.4
$21,600–$24,500	6.1	7.0	2.3	8.9	10.3	1.7	5.0	5.2	3.9	1.8	2.2	0.5
$24,600 or more	9.7	10.8	5.4	14.1	16.0	4.6	7.9	8.4	6.0	3.5	2.9	5.6
Salary basis:												
9/10 months	66.8	66.2	69.0	60.1	69.3	64.3	68.4	68.7	67.5	78.9	78.5	79.9
11/12 months	33.2	33.8	31.0	39.9	40.7	35.7	31.6	31.3	32.5	21.1	21.5	20.1

professional faculties in which women were marginal at best.

One analysis by Jessie Bernard suggests that women are represented in college faculties in roughly the same proportion as in the qualified labor force of women with five or more years of college. If doctors' degrees are used as the criterion of qualification, according to this analysis, then women are actually over-represented in college faculties, since only 10 percent of doctorates are held by women, and many of these are not in the labor force. "If the proportion of academic people who are women seems small, it is in part at least because the proportion of women in the qualified labor force is small."

Qualification is a two-way street, however. Women are less likely to become full professors because they are less likely to have doctorates, but they are also less likely to pursue doctorates because it is so difficult for them to penetrate the ranks of the tenured full professors. It is also, of course, difficult for them to penetrate the departments and faculties that admit Ph.D. candidates and award them doctorates.

The Earnings Gap

The average salary of women faculty is only about 83 percent of male salary. In 1969, for example, 28 percent of faculty men and 63 percent of faculty women were paid less than $10,000 a year. Women earn less because they are at lower faculty ranks and because they are paid less than men of the same rank. The earnings gap tends to increase with rank. Among instructors, assistant professors, and associate professors, the gap was found to be $500, in favor of male faculty. At the rank of full professor, the gap was $1,400, also in favor of males.

Status

A study of the academic marketplace late in the fifties concluded that women scholars are not taken seriously and cannot look forward to a normal professional career. Women tend to be discriminated against, the study found, not because they have low prestige but because they are outside the prestige system entirely.

Even college women reveal prejudices against academic women and what they produce. In one experiment, college women were given sets of articles in various professional fields, written by three males and three females. When the authors' names were switched, it was found that articles bearing the names of male authors were rated higher on all criteria of excellence (value, persuasiveness, profundity, style, competence) than when the same articles bore the names of female authors. Even articles on homemaking and dietetics were rated higher when they bore the name of a male author.

While such prejudicial responses probably declined during the seventies, much residual prejudice may remain among both sexes about the intellectual "authority" of academic women.

Administration

Only a few four-year coeducational colleges have women presidents. Even of the nonchurch women's schools, only eight had women presidents in 1971. None of the fifty largest college libraries is headed by a woman, although women librarians are abundant. Only a few academic deans are women, although there are many deans of women. Most schools of social work now have male deans, although a number of women headed these schools in the past. While women are as much as a quarter of all faculty, they are only 17 percent of administrators and 13 percent of members of governing boards in higher education.

Characteristics

"Pieced together from a wide variety of sources," says Jessie Bernard in *Academic Women,* "the model

Table 16. Demographic and Background Characteristics of College Faculty Members, by Type of Institution and by Sex: United States, Spring, 1969
[Percentage Distribution]

Item	All Institutions			Universities			Four-Year Colleges			Two-Year Colleges		
	Total	Men	Women	Total	Men	Women	Total	Men	Women	Total	Men	Women
1	2	3	4	5	6	7	8	9	10	11	12	13
Total	100.0	100.0	100.0	100.0	100.0	100.0	100.0	100.0	100.0	100.0	100.0	100.0
Age:												
Over 60 (born before 1909)	7.7	7.3	9.3	7.4	7.2	8.6	8.5	7.9	10.4	6.6	6.2	8.0
51-60 (born 1909-1918)	15.7	15.1	18.5	15.7	15.1	19.4	15.6	15.0	17.7	16.1	15.2	18.5
41-50 (born 1919-1928)	26.7	26.7	26.6	27.1	27.3	25.8	25.7	25.6	26.4	28.0	27.6	29.0
36-40 (born 1929-1933)	16.5	17.3	13.0	17.3	18.3	11.7	15.9	16.4	14.5	14.6	15.5	12.2
31-35 (born 1934-1938)	17.4	18.5	12.8	17.8	18.6	13.3	17.1	18.4	12.8	16.6	18.3	11.9
30 or less (born after 1938)	16.0	15.0	19.7	14.6	13.4	21.1	17.0	16.7	18.1	18.0	17.2	20.3
Race:												
White	96.3	96.6	94.7	97.7	97.7	97.7	93.5	94.2	91.3	98.4	99.1	96.7
Black	2.2	1.8	3.9	0.5	0.4	1.0	5.0	4.2	7.4	.7	.5	1.4
Oriental	1.3	1.3	1.1	1.6	1.6	1.0	1.2	1.2	.9	.5	.2	1.4
Other	.3	.3	.3	.3	.3	.2	.4	.4	.3	.3	.2	.5
Citizenship												
Not U.S. citizen	3.8	4.0	2.8	4.8	5.1	3.1	3.3	3.3	3.2	.9	.8	1.3
U.S. citizen, naturalized	5.3	5.5	4.6	5.6	5.6	5.3	5.6	5.8	4.9	3.8	4.3	2.2
U.S. citizen, native	90.9	90.5	92.6	89.6	89.2	91.6	91.1	90.9	91.9	95.3	94.8	96.5
Father's educational attainment:												
Eighth grade or less	29.1	30.0	25.6	26.1	26.9	21.9	30.5	31.5	26.7	37.1	39.4	30.5
Some high school	14.3	14.4	13.7	13.5	13.6	13.3	15.0	15.4	13.6	15.1	15.2	15.0
Completed high school	17.5	17.5	17.4	17.3	17.2	17.7	17.1	17.4	16.0	19.3	19.1	20.1

Some college	12.6	12.4	13.7	13.1	12.9	14.2	12.2	12.2	12.3	12.1	10.8	15.9
College graduate	9.7	9.6	10.0	11.0	10.9	11.7	9.0	8.7	10.1	6.5	6.7	5.8
Some graduate school	5.4	5.0	7.1	5.8	5.5	7.5	5.6	4.9	7.8	3.2	2.7	4.5
Advanced degree	11.4	11.1	12.6	13.1	13.0	13.8	10.7	9.9	13.3	6.6	6.1	8.2
Religious background:												
Protestant	64.1	63.9	65.4	67.6	66.8	72.2	59.4	59.3	59.7	64.3	64.4	64.1
Catholic	16.9	15.9	21.3	13.0	12.7	14.8	19.9	18.6	24.3	23.4	21.8	28.2
Jewish	9.7	10.4	6.7	10.1	10.7	6.2	11.5	12.3	8.9	3.3	3.7	2.2
Other	3.3	3.4	2.7	3.3	3.4	2.6	3.2	3.3	2.9	3.6	3.8	2.8
None	3.2	3.3	2.6	3.7	3.7	3.3	2.9	3.1	2.5	2.2	2.4	1.4
No answer	2.7	3.0	1.2	2.3	2.6	.9	3.0	3.4	1.6	3.1	3.8	1.3
Current religion:												
Protestant	47.9	47.1	51.4	48.9	47.8	55.8	45.1	44.6	46.7	52.0	51.4	53.5
Catholic	13.5	12.2	19.2	9.6	9.2	12.2	16.4	14.7	22.4	20.1	17.8	26.8
Jewish	7.0	7.3	5.4	6.9	7.3	4.9	8.6	9.0	7.5	2.4	2.6	1.6
Other	5.9	6.1	5.2	6.0	6.2	5.1	5.6	5.7	5.1	6.8	7.1	5.9
None	20.7	21.9	15.6	23.7	24.6	18.8	19.0	20.2	15.0	13.8	15.0	10.1
No answer	4.9	5.4	3.1	4.7	4.9	3.4	5.3	5.8	3.3	5.0	6.0	2.1
Martial status:												
Currently married	79.3	87.0	47.4	83.2	89.4	48.1	74.9	83.7	45.6	76.7	86.0	50.3
Divorced, separated, widowed	4.8	3.0	12.4	4.1	2.7	12.1	5.7	3.5	12.9	5.2	2.8	12.2
Never married	15.9	10.0	40.1	12.7	7.9	39.8	19.4	12.8	41.5	18.1	11.2	37.5
Number of children:												
None	36.1	29.3	65.3	32.3	26.2	67.3	40.6	33.7	64.8	38.0	29.7	61.9
One	15.9	16.7	12.3	15.7	16.4	12.0	16.0	16.9	12.8	16.3	18.0	11.5
Two	23.7	26.3	12.9	25.4	27.7	12.0	22.0	24.3	13.8	22.5	25.9	12.7
Three or more	24.3	27.7	9.6	26.6	29.7	8.7	21.4	25.1	8.6	23.1	26.3	13.9

NOTE.—Data are based upon a sample survey by the Carnegie Commission on the Future of Higher Education and the American Council on Education. Because of rounding, percentages may not add to 100.0.

SOURCE: American Council on Education, Research Report Vol.5, No. 5, *College and University Faculty: A Statistical Description*, June 1970.

picture of the academic woman that emerges is of a very bright person so far as test intelligence is concerned, but compliant rather than aggressive, from an above-average social class background, and with a major interest in the humanities." The more contemporary woman academician is probably at least somewhat less compliant.

More female than male academicians are 51 years and over (28 percent and 22 percent). Fewer possess the doctorate (25 percent of females and 50 percent of males). Fewer are married (47 percent of females and 87 percent of males). More than two in three women academicians have no children (67.3 percent), compared with 26.2 percent of males.

Bernard speculates that this plethora of spinsters is accounted for by the academic monastic tradition (which segregates domestic and scholastic life), a preference for celibacy, and the shortage of qualified spouses.

"The academic woman," says Bernard, "is the woman who has time for her students, time to sponsor organizations, time to talk to them. She is the woman without competing demands from husband or children. She is, almost without any doubt, in professional status—as evidenced by her large average membership in professional societies—and her major interest is almost certainly teaching, not research."

Almost three in four women faculty at universities, as distinguished from two- or four-year colleges, are Protestant in religious background (72 percent). Protestantism is more common among women than among male academics, and faculty with Catholic backgrounds are significantly under-represented among both sexes at the university level, but more so among males than among females.

Hence, the middle-aged Protestant spinster or childless woman is a common figure among women university faculty members.

Productivity

In academia, rewards and merit ratings are usually based on several criteria, the most important of which is research and publication. The idea is that the highest function of the scholar is not to pass on to students knowledge developed by others—to teach—but to develop new knowledge, through research and reflection, and impart that knowledge to others through publications.

Various studies suggest that academic women may be less productive, in this sense, than their male counterparts.

Some explanations of this lower productivity assert that women produce and create less because they are less daring, original, competitive, or contentious. Other explanations turn to the proven bias against the writings and authority of women, the difficulties women experience in getting their work published, probable bias in the awarding of research funds, and the general cultural and academic context in which research and writing are done.

Women may, indeed, write less because they are more rather than less gifted and productive writers and researchers. They may feel uncomfortable with the style of inquiry in their discipline, the lack of significance in research undertaken, or the special language, jargon, and obscurantisms that may mark academic prose. A case in point may be Barbara Tuchman, a brilliant and distinguished writer and scholar who has been only reluctantly recognized by historians. Had she come up through the academic discipline, she may never have produced so prolifically and with such extraordinary results.

Academic women suffer certain disadvantages because they are not taken seriously by peers, but they may also enjoy certain advantages because of it. They can get away with more, do the unexpected and unorthodox, be more radical and outspoken without notice or criticism. Because they *are* outside the status system, women are less threatening to the men who run higher education. That is one thing to be grateful for.

Law

13

The Law: Toward Equal Protection

The effort to reduce discrimination in schools and other social institutions has been aided in a dramatic way by the adoption of federal law and by the willingness of some courts to enforce the constitutional guarantees of equal protection.

So active has the law become in recent years, and so voluminous the court cases, that the average citizen, untrained in the labyrinths and language of the law, may retreat before the proliferation of clauses, amendments, acts, agencies, enforcement procedures, federal, state, and local versions of similar laws.

The proposed Equal Rights Amendment to the United States Constitution will try to diminish this confusion by making it clearly unconstitutional to deny equal rights to citizens based on sex.

With respect to schools, sex discrimination has to a large extent been prohibited—and certainly the issues have been clarified—by a federal law which was made effective on July 21, 1975. This landmark law is the so-called Title IX of the Education Amendments of 1972.

Students and employees in educational institutions who seek redress from discriminatory practices are now covered, in specified cases, by the following laws of the land:

1. Title IX of the Education Amendments of 1972.
2. Titles VII and VIII of the Public Health Service Act for people in the health professions.

3. Amendments to the Equal Pay Act and Title VII of the 1964 Civil Rights Act—to include protection for teachers and other school employees against sex discrimination.

4. Equal rights laws adopted in some states.

5. Last, but far from least, the Equal Protection clause of the Fourteenth Amendment to the United States Constitution—and perhaps at some future date, the Equal Rights Amendment to the Constitution.

In general, however, Title IX, if properly enforced (and eventually expanded) will go a long way toward ending sex discrimination in educational institutions, for both students and employees.

The title depends for enforcement only on the denial of federal funds to discriminating schools, a penalty of considerable weight. It cannot, however, offer protection against discrimination among schools that choose to forego federal funds rather than cease discriminatory practices. Only constitutional guarantees are now, to some extent, able to do that.

Title IX of the Educational Amendments of 1972

Since 1964 and the historic passage of the Civil Rights Act, federal law has prohibited sex discrimination in employment, and the Equal Employment Opportunities Commission (EEOC) of the United States Department of Labor has enforced the law. Unfortunately, the law has not until recently applied to employment in educational institutions.

Title IX of the Educational Amendments will apply not only to employees but also to students in educational institutions. It is by far the broadest and most comprehensive of the sex discrimination laws affecting schools. The interpretation of the law and its enforcement will be within the jurisdiction of the U.S. Department of Health, Education, and Welfare.

Though Title IX was adopted into law in June, 1972, it was not made effective by HEW until July 21, 1975.

Some critics take this three-year delay as evidence of the formidable resistance that exists in the education establishment, and particularly among male administrators and professionals, to the prohibition of sex discrimination in the schools. It remains to be seen whether such resistance will be evidenced in the enforcement of the law.

Title IX specifies, "No person in the United States shall, on the basis of sex, be excluded from participation in, be denied the benefits of, or be subjected to discrimination under any education program or activity receiving Federal financial assistance." The law applies to almost all public school systems and postsecondary schools, including 16,000 public school systems throughout the nation and almost 2,700 postsecondary schools. Military schools are completely exempted, as are religious schools where compliance would be inconsistent with religious tenets. Some other institutions have limited exemptions.

With respect to school admissions (but not other parts of the law) the final regulations adopted by HEW apply only to vocational, professional, and graduate schools, and to public undergraduate schools, except those that have been traditionally and continually open to one sex only. The regulations on admissions do not apply to preschools, elementary and secondary schools, private undergraduate schools, or public undergraduate schools that have always discriminated. However, even schools whose admissions practices are exempt are prohibited from practicing sex discrimination once students of both sexes have been admitted.

Issues

The six major public issues in connection with the adoption of the final HEW regulations on the law were:

1. Physical Education Classes. The regulations permit

separation of the sexes for contact sports, the grouping of students by physical and athletic ability, and attendance at sex education classes. At all other times physical education must be coeducational under the regulations.

2. Financial Aid. The regulations prohibit schools from administering scholarships that designate a particular sex as recipient unless such scholarships are "pooled." Two steps are required for pooling. Step one requires that schools select students for financial awards on a basis other than a student's sex. Step two requires that, once selected, male and female students should receive proportional awards, drawing on both sex-restricted and non-sex-restricted funds.

3. Foreign Scholarships. The regulations do not prohibit schools from administering single-sex scholarships or awards given under foreign wills, trusts, or similar legal instruments for study abroad, provided the school also makes available reasonable foreign study opportunities to students of the other sex.

4. Pension Benefits. The regulations allow schools to provide either equal contributions or equal periodic benefits to males and females under pension plans. Many school pension plans, but relatively few in other types of employment, pay women lower monthly benefits after retirement than they pay men, even though contributions are the same. Title IX does not change this discriminatory practice.

5. Curriculum and Textbooks. The regulations do not cover sex stereotyping in textbooks or curriculum materials.

6. Athletics. The regulations require that schools provide equal opportunity for both sexes to participate in intramural, interscholastic, and intercollegiate athletics. The sex segregation of teams is allowed, however, in contact sports and in sports where competitive skill is the basis for selecting team members. This includes virtually all teams.

Equalized funds are not required, but failure to provide necessary funds for one sex will be taken into account in assessing equality of opportunity. Among factors to be considered in deciding if equal athletic opportunities are available are:

1. Whether the sports selected by the school reflect the interests and abilities of both sexes.

2. The provision of supplies and equipment to participants.

3. Travel and per diem allowances given to athletes.

4. The scheduling of games and practice.

5. Opportunities available for coaching in athletics and for tutoring in academic subjects—and the assignment and pay of coaches and tutors.

6. Medical and training services offered to participants.

7. Locker rooms and practice facilities.

8. Housing and dining facilities and services.

9. Publicity given to athletic events.

If noncontact teams, such as tennis, are offered for men and not for women, then women are entitled to compete for a place on the male team. Schools are required to provide separate teams in contact and noncontact sports where the provision of only one team would not "accommodate the interests and abilities of members of both sexes."

Elementary schools have one year to comply with these regulations and secondary and postsecondary schools have three years.

Though these have been the most controversial issues, especially the regulation on athletics, the essential core of Title IX applies mainly to discrimination in admissions and in employment.

Admissions

The quotas and higher standards that have limited

female enrollment in graduate school programs are prohibited by Title IX.

The regulations prohibit separate ranking of applicants, sex quotas, administration of sex-biased tests, and the granting of preference to applicants based on attendance at particular schools if the preference results in discrimination.

The regulations forbid any discriminatory application of rules on marital or parental status or pregnancy—provided such pregnancy is treated as a temporary disability.

The recruitment of students is covered, as well as admission practices. Comparable efforts must be made to recruit members of each sex. Where sex discrimination has existed, additional recruitment efforts are required to remedy the effects of discrimination.

Treatment

While some schools are exempt from regulations on admissions, all schools are required to treat students, once admitted, without discrimination on the basis of sex. Specifically, the treatment requirements apply to:

1. Participation in all courses offered and all extracurricular activities.

2. Participation in benefits, services, and financial aid.

3. The use of school facilities and the comparability of housing rules and facilities. (Single sex housing is permitted, however).

Schools are prohibited from providing significant assistance to professional or honorary fraternal organizations that discriminate on the basis of sex. The regulations (by specific congressional act in 1974) exempt the membership practices of fraternities and sororities in higher education, and youth organizations such as the Scouts and the Y.W.C.A.

Examples of treatment:

1. A school may not allow only boys to take shop

and only girls to take home economics, or operate separate classes in these subjects for boys and girls.

2. Schools may not discriminate in vocational counseling. Generally, the same testing and guidance materials should be used.

3. Schools may not segregate boys and girls into different physical education classes.

4. A school that has one swimming pool must make it equally available to males and females.

Employment

All employees in all institutions are covered, including all part-time employees and instructional, administrative, maintenance, and other employees. The only schools exempted are military schools and religious schools where compliance would be inconsistent with religious tenets.

Employment policies generally will follow those of the Equal Employment Opportunity Commission, which requires nondiscrimination in employment criteria, recruitment, compensation, job classification and structure, fringe benefits, marital or parental status, advertising of jobs, and handling of pre-employment inquiries. Leaves of absence and fringe benefits must be offered to pregnant employees as they are offered to the temporarily disabled.

Notes

Title IX is especially useful to women because it covers all school employees, including teachers, researchers, teacher aides, secretaries, service workers, supervision. Because of its broad coverage it can bring women together across the occupational and class lines that usually limit communication among them. The effectiveness of the law, however, will depend very much on how much staff HEW will have to enforce it and how willing it will be to terminate aid to offending institutions.

Women or men wishing to file complaints under Title IX should write a detailed letter to the Director of the Office of Civil Rights, Department of Health, Education, and Welfare, Washington, D.C. A source of technical information and assistance in discrimination by postsecondary schools is The Project on the Status and Education of Women, Association of American Colleges, 1818 R Street, N.W., Washington, D.C. 20009.

The exemption under Title IX of religious and military schools is particularly important because it applies so specifically to the male domination of social institutions. Sex discrimination by religious faiths and schools often provides the ideology and rationale for sex discrimination in society and in its social institutions. As guardians of moral and ethical codes and of other-worldly rewards, religious institutions, in their own beliefs and practices, can in effect sanction and legitimate discrimination in other institutions, as well as in the hearts and minds of those subject to their teachings.

Military schools, also exempt from Title IX coverage, are the guardians not of the beliefs but of the physical power in society and of the ultimate weapons of domination. While military academies which train military leadership have begun to open their doors to women, the lack of access to these academies contributes in a significant way to the exclusion of women from this and other male-dominated policy centers of the society.

Similarly, the private prep schools and the private undergraduate colleges (such as the Ivy League schools), which are exempt from the admissions requirements of the law, have trained students for participation in the policy-making elites of the society. If these schools continue to discriminate, women will continue to be excluded from the leadership roles for which males are prepared in these schools.

In the long run, however, it is likely that many

of these exempt institutions will conform voluntarily
to the requirements of the law as they see other schools
moving rapidly in that direction.

The Public Health Services Act

Besides Title IX, students in the health professions
have recourse to the Public Health Service Act in cases
of sex discrimination. Two sections of that act (799A
and 845) prohibit schools that receive federal aid under
Titles VII and VIII of the Public Health Service
Act—the vast majority of schools—from practicing sex
discrimination. The act applies also to hospitals that
operate medical schools or training programs. Medical
schools under the act may not set quotas on women,
as most have done in the past, and they may not refuse
to admit people over 30 if such refusal results in
discrimination (as in the case of women who reenter
school after their families are raised).

Those in the health professions who are not helped
by Title IX because of its numerous exceptions (as
in the case of admissions to private undergraduate
schools) may seek assistance under this act. Preferably,
they will seek assistance under both acts.

The enforcement penalty is the withdrawal of federal
aid. Aid will be withdrawn in three cases: if the school
fails to provide assurances that it will not discriminate,
or if, in conducting its routine investigations, HEW
finds discrimination, or if, after complaints are received and reviewed by HEW, discrimination is found.
Complaints may be filed by sending a letter with
detailed charges to the Director of the Office of Civil
Rights, Department of Health, Education, and Welfare,Washington, D.C., and federal courts may be
called upon to review HEW action.

Amendments to the Equal Pay Act and the Civil Rights Act

Both the Equal Pay Act and the 1964 Civil Rights
Act, which previously exempted teachers, have been

amended to protect them against sex discrimination.
Teachers may now sue in federal court to force schools
to adopt nondiscriminatory practices and to recover
wages they may have lost because of discriminatory
practices.

These amendments are more beneficial to teachers
in private schools since teachers in public schools
have a right to sue in federal courts under the equal
protection clause of the Fourteenth Amendment to
the Constitution.

State Laws

Some states (as Alaska, Illinois, Indiana, Massachusetts, New York) also have equal rights laws. These
laws, which are of varying usefulness, can also be
called upon to enforce nondiscriminatory practices in
schools.

The Equal Protection Clause of the Fourteenth
Amendment to the U.S. Constitution

The equal protection clause of the Fourteenth
Amendment says: "No State shall . . . deny to any
person within its jurisdiction the equal protection of
the laws."

This clause can be used against discrimination by
state and local laws. In effect, women may sue any
public school supported by local or state funds (elementary, secondary, and postsecondary) under the
equal protection clause. No private institutions are
covered.

Since the clause is not interpreted uniformly by
the courts, the outcome of such suits is often uncertain.
Suits to admit females to the prestigious University
of Virginia at Charlottesville, Stuyvesant High School
in New York City, and the Boston Latin schools were
successful in the courts. Other suits, such as those
filed against Texas A & M, were unsuccessful, although

in the end the school voluntarily opened its admissions to women students.

The Equal Rights Amendment to the Constitution, if passed, will clarify and expand the constitutional coverage. Its language will read: "Equality of rights under the law shall not be denied or abridged by the United States or by any State on account of sex."

Vocations and Beyond

14

Studies For and About Women:
Policies and Politics

As women have grown more aware of their common interests, they have increasingly organized to advance them. Many women have come to view themselves as an oppressed and exploited minority, sharing the disadvantaged status of racial and ethnic minorities. Other women view themselves as essentially privileged, but nonetheless sharing common interests that can be advanced, like those of bankers and businessmen, by moderate forms of collective action.

The continuum of awareness or discontent runs from politicized feminists at one end to a much larger group that simply seeks some measure of advancement. Outside this continuum are women, perhaps a majority, who are either neutral or hostile to major changes in women's status—or who are simply uninformed about the nature of proposed change.

These strands of sentiment give rise to a variety of innovative school programs, almost all of them in higher education. Most are designed either to teach special groups of women or to teach women about women. This women's movement has had virtually no impact on primary or secondary schools, except insofar as law may affect sex-segregated programs.

The two major innovations are women's studies and continuing education for mature women. Women's studies usually aim to teach women about women,

much as Black Studies teach blacks about their own
history, achievements, and needs. The newer continuing education programs offer mature women (a significant new group in education) vocational preparation
and self-enrichment. These women may also, of course,
engage in women's studies.

The term women's studies, however, is also often
applied to research about women and even to regular
instruction offered to women. Implicit in the term
is the concept of consciousness raising and the view
of women as a separate group which has unique needs
and disadvantages, in school and elsewhere.

Continuing Education

Special programs have been created in many places
to deal with a labor market phenomenon of rather
recent vintage—the return of mature women to the
job market after having spent at least several years
in child rearing. In previous generations, families
tended to be so large, women so relatively short-lived,
and job opportunities for mature women so scarce,
that such reentry of women into the labor force was
uncommon.

Between 1950 and 1969, women in the labor force
increased by twelve million, 62 percent of whom were
older than 35 years of age. Among the age groups,
the greatest gain in employment during recent decades
has been made by women age 45 to 54. In 1940,
25 percent of women in this age group were employed;
in 1950 the figure was 37 percent and in 1969, it
was 54 percent.

Most of these mature women needed education and
training to prepare them for the job market. The need
was highlighted by the rise in school enrollments of
women age 25 to 29 from 26,000 to 311,000 between
1950 and 1969—and of women age 30 to 34, from
21,000 to 215,000.

The college programs created to offer special
preparation for mature women provide both liberal

arts and more vocationally oriented education. These programs, in their special structure and content, stress the value of association with age peers, the scheduling of classes to meet special student needs, the importance of counseling—and in many cases, job placement, financial aid, liberal transfer credit, and even credit for life experience.

The first of these new continuing education programs for women was created after World War II and tried to provide intensive teacher training for women with liberal arts degrees.

Following a few experimental efforts in the fifties, some of the larger colleges and universities began to initiate programs.

In 1960 the University of Minnesota set up a center that organized the resources of the university for adult women. The object of the program was to help women reach their goals, whatever they were—careers, self-enrichment, community participation. Guidance was the core feature of the program. Women entered existing university programs suitable to their individualized goals and participated in several one-year seminars, scheduled for three morning hours every other week. They also participated in reading, study skills, and guidance seminars and in noncredit courses, some of which met in students' homes and off-campus.

The Radcliffe Institute for Independent Study was begun at about the same time. In the beginning the program served only women with degrees who needed an opportunity to do creative work. Later the Institute also offered regular liberal arts courses to mature women.

Rutgers University initiated a program in 1961 to train women college graduates in mathematics. The program, aimed at relieving the shortage of math teachers, involved about 600 women students by 1968.

Another early program was started in 1961 at the University of Kansas City, offering noncredit seminars for women in liberal arts and women's studies.

Sarah Lawrence began a program for undergraduate
and graduate women in 1962, involving special counseling and cooperative programs with other colleges
in the New York vicinity.

Students in these programs tend to be women of
middle or upper-middle income, many with previous
college experience. Typically, they are married to men
in professional or managerial occupations and are
active in community organizations.

Despite their generally high educational levels, most
were found to lack confidence on their initial contact
with the college, so that the reception they had was
especially important to their adjustment. Women report
that their children also profit from their participation
in these programs, in that they develop more interests,
take on more responsibilities, and benefit from their
mothers' achievements and gratifications.

Concern has grown about offering similar services
to women other than suburban housewives, women
whose educational needs are still unmet—especially
working class and low-income women, working
women, women with young children, and women who
have lost their husbands and need to support themselves.

Postsecondary continuing education programs may
receive federal aid under the Community Service and
Continuing Education Programs, covered by Title I
of the Higher Education Act of 1965. The object of
this aid program is "to apply the resources of institutions of higher education, both public and private,
to the solution of community problems by enlarging
and extending university extension and continuing
education programs. . . . Community problems of
concern are health, jobs, recreation, housing, transit,
poverty, crime, etc."

Programs for mature women, like most training
programs, have tended to flourish during times of full
employment, when the demand for trained workers
is high. It remains to be seen what effects economic

recession may have on such programs.

Colleges may seek mature women even when employers do not. Certainly colleges are highly motivated to find new student populations. This is especially true when recessions affect their finances and when student enrollments drop because of declines in the college-age group.

Mature women are everywhere prime candidates for recruitment into special college programs. If they are housewives, they simply have more time for studies than do their employed husbands. Whether women, when job opportunities decline, will have the same incentives to enter such programs, is a matter for speculation.

Adult Education

The programs previously discussed are only the fast-growing edge of an elaborate and long established system of continuing education, mainly in postsecondary schools, and adult education, offered mainly in secondary evening schools. More women than men now participate in adult education programs and the increase in their participation has been twice the rate of males. A total of more than thirteen million people take part in what is classified by the U.S. Office of Education as adult education, and the costs of these programs exceed $130 million a year.

This network of programs and courses is far too massive and complex to be treated in this volume, though it is clearly a suitable subject for further inquiry. Such a discussion is omitted in the present context, however, mainly because so few of these courses have apparently been designed either for or about women—aside from the traditional home economics offerings. Little publicity is given to women's courses in adult education because they serve mainly noncollege women who have a low profile on the women's scene and in the media.

These programs have a potential for reaching deep

into the communities of noncollege women, where the vast majority of American women live, and bringing to them skills and knowledge they can use to improve themselves, their families, communities, and the status of women generally.

In the past, adult education has too often focused on courses, subject matter, and narrowly vocational subjects—usually of a highly traditional nature—to the neglect of people and their needs, as individuals, groups, and communities. Rarely have adult education programs addressed themselves to the special needs of women, as an interest group, as a "minority," as people who can play a significant role, collectively, in consumer affairs, civic and community affairs, the world of work and of politics.

Women's Studies

Women's studies, like ethnic studies, tend to deal with the culture, status, development, and achievements of women as a group. The San Diego State College program in women's studies, approved in 1970, was reportedly the first of its kind. A year later there were fifteen women's studies programs in higher education and more than 600 courses offered in more than 200 postsecondary schools. By 1973 there were more than 1,200 courses, and the numbers, as listed by the Clearinghouse on Women's Studies, were growing rapidly.

Very few of these courses have been offered to prospective teachers in schools of education who could, in turn, pass their knowledge and awareness of women's issues on to their students.

The women's studies movement has been created largely by and for younger women. Active participants tend to be more career than family oriented, though courses center more on women as a subject than on strict vocationalism. Many of the most active participants are undoubtedly the daughters and kin of the suburban housewives who enroll in continuing education programs or of the academic and professional women who made their break from suburban domestic life somewhat earlier.

So great has been the demand of women for courses specifically addressed to them that even many small, private initiatives have thrived. A case in point is the Womanschool, a small independent, nonprofit school, opened in 1975 to provide practical studies for women. Its aims were modest: to recruit a few teachers with a newspaper ad and hold classes in someone's home. The advertisement received 400 responses. A small catalog was printed and 5,000 requests for it were received within weeks. A classroom was rented in a New York college and the school opened with almost 600 registered students (at tuition of $70 per credit point). Among the courses offered were "Women in Management," "How to Manage your Own Financial Affairs," "Great Part-time Jobs and How to Get Them"; no feminist studies or women's studies were included. The school is not accredited, but credit for attendance is given at a few institutions where the same students are also enrolled.

Directions

The experiences of these special programs for and about women indicate the need for change in regular academic and professional programs at the under-graduate and graduate levels. Especially important to the fuller and more successful participation of women in these programs are: 1) class scheduling suited to the needs of housewives; 2) academic and vocational counseling; 3) part-time graduate studies; 4) a stan-dardized system which will permit full transfer of credits earned in other institutions; 5) the abolition of time limits on credits earned; 6) outreach—to recruit, welcome, and orient women into predominantly male studies; 7) credit for life experience; 8) credit for independent study, correspondence in lieu of class attendance, television instruction; 9) the optional sub-

stitution of tests and examinations for class attendance;
10) the organization of women's clubs within the field
of study or profession; 11) the substitution of weekend
or one-week seminars for daily or weekly class attendance.

In graduate and professional schools, women have,
through the organization of groups within schools and
professions, sought to open professional training in
nontraditional occupations to larger numbers of
women.

The concept of the open university and the university
without walls gives women (and men) an opportunity
to shape their school hours to their work and domestic
obligations. An open university such as the national
one in Britain, whose success is now proven, permits
television and correspondence instruction, combined
with examinations and limited scheduled meetings
with teachers and seminar groups.

General Education Development tests, offering the
equivalent of a high school diploma, and the College
Level Examination Program of the College Entrance
Examination Board have validated the awarding of
credit by examination in lieu of class attendance.
Examinations in other specific subject matter, offered
in secondary and postsecondary schools, would give
women (and men) further relief from the obligations
of class attendance.

Beyond these efforts to make education more attrac-
tive, available, and financially feasible for women lies
a question relating to the vocational function of education: the unsettled matter of the suitability of *any*
schooling to the actual performance of *any* job. The
matter is unsettled because so little research has been
done on this vital question and because the courts
are not yet clear in their rulings. The main question
is: Can employers and job training programs require
applicants to submit school credentials that have no
proven effect on job performance?

Nor has the equally vital question of the relevance

of specific school requirements for occupational licenses been more than superficially explored.

These matters were first brought into general discussion, and into the courts, by the civil rights movement and by blacks who felt they could perform certain jobs for which they lacked school credentials. While women generally have higher educational levels than blacks, they are still handicapped by some of the artificial school requirements of many jobs, such as some of those that require the Ph.D.

We have given extensive attention in this volume to the ways in which women may prosper vocationally through the equalization of educational opportunity, adaptation of schools to the special needs of women, and the socialization of women from early childhood for group and collective activity and for roles of leadership and authority. We have also given some attention to the job market itself, to the favorable impact of full employment on women, the need to enforce the law against job discrimination, and the need to restructure occupations and hours of employment to meet the special needs of women with families, not to mention the vast national need for child care facilities.

Still, much remains unsaid. Indeed, a whole, highly sensitive area of women's activity and educational need is unexplored. This area has to do with women's domestic role. In this volume we have seen that women have assumed, or been assigned, a variety of roles throughout recorded history. These roles include: sexual and reproductive; menial service functions, as cleaning clothes, dishes, living quarters; skilled domestic tasks, as spinning, weaving, making clothing; skilled agrarian labor, as gardening and raising small livestock. Among the most socially valuable and historically advanced roles women have assumed has been the rearing and instruction of the young. This responsibility led eventually to the professional emancipation of women through teaching.

The contemporary world, however, has at one and
the same time made the domestic role of women both
simpler and, at least potentially, more complex. The
vast array of household labor-saving devices has greatly reduced the amount of simple, menial, hard work
that housewives must do. At the same time, events
and the complexities of modern life have greatly
increased her actual, and possible, home-community-
society roles.

An event of the last century that is certainly of equal
significance to the growth of the economic independence of women and the performance of work roles
outside the home has been the extension of the rights
of full citizenship to women, including the right to
vote and run for political office. In a sense, the
housewife is especially well situated, in many cases,
to perform these civic and political roles. Simply
enough, she usually has more time, if her children
are in school, than does the working woman. Not only
is she better able than the working woman or man
to carry on community and political activities, but
such activities are particularly well suited to her own
need for highly flexible, self-arranged work hours. She
can also assume with some confidence that such
community functions are congruent with home and
family functions, since they directly affect the welfare
of community members.

Moreover, it is hardly an exaggeration to say that
the ultimate source of authority and social power in
a democratic society lies in politics and public law,
for these are the control centers of all other economic,
educational, social, and cultural activities. Women who
are unable to influence or reach the highest levels
of authority in schools or in business and industry,
can, through politics, gain access to all this and more.

It is only regrettable that schools do so little to
inform women politically, to teach them skills useful
in community and political activity, to go much beyond
the narrow and highly traditional confines of home

economics. Concerns for the domestic roles of women have rarely even led to participation in the highly successful, valuable, and complex consumers' movement, with all its implications for family life and the general social welfare.

At some future time, it may be that most women will choose work roles over domestic roles, if opportunities are available to do so. Even in that event, however, the interim period may still find a majority of women functioning in mainly domestic roles. Given that fact, would it not be worthwhile for educators and women activists to examine the ways in which that domestic role may be enlarged and enriched for the betterment of both housewives and society?

If we choose to move in this direction, perhaps we might also turn more attention to another neglected female majority—the noncollege woman and the working class woman.

College women, professional women, and suburban housewives have made valuable contributions to the sexual democratization of our society, but to ensure the completion of that democratization as well as the reduction of even higher class barriers, suggests a need to direct far more public resources to noncollege women.

Strides in this direction may be made by introducing women's studies into the schools of education that train the teachers of noncollege women, and into the elementary and secondary schools themselves, where these noncollege women are enrolled.

The school, in its symbiotic relationship with women over the years, has benefited women in their roles as mothers enabling them to teach and guide their own children. It has benefited them in their roles as workers, to the extent that it has supervised their children while they work, offered them rewarding jobs within the schools, broadened their intellectual horizons, raised their aspirations, and given them the certificates and vocational preparation that employers seek. It has also benefited women to some extent in their roles as community participants and leaders.

Discrimination and sex-role typing, especially in higher education and vocational education, have handicapped women in their pursuit of equal opportunities, but the law, the vigilance of women, and even the consent of men, promise a major readjustment of these imbalances. Women are no longer the giddy, gossipy creatures described in pre-industrial essays. Their work and their education have changed their role, their character, and their consciousness. Nor are the schools what they once were, before the advent of the educated woman.

Appendix A. Bachelor's, Master's, and Doctor's Degrees Conferred by Institutions of Higher Education, by Sex of Student and by Field of Study: United States, 1970-71

Major field of study	Bachelor's degrees requiring 4 or 5 years			Second level (master's) degrees			Doctor's degrees (Ph.D., Ed.D., etc.)		
	Total	Men	Women	Total	Men	Women	Total	Men	Women
1	2	3	4	5	6	7	8	9	10
All fields	839,730	476,584	364,136	230,509	138,146	92,363	32,107	27,530	4,577
Agriculture and natural resources	12,672	12,136	536	2,457	2,313	144	1,086	1,055	31
Agriculture, general	1,491	1,445	46	123	122	1	—	—	—
Agronomy	823	812	11	293	283	10	169	165	4
Soils science	212	207	5	87	84	3	89	84	5
Animal science	2,445	2,222	223	344	318	26	145	140	5
Dairy science	245	237	8	54	52	2	30	30	—
Poultry science	80	79	1	50	45	5	27	27	—
Fish, game, and wildlife management	936	916	20	151	144	7	43	42	1
Horticulture	385	347	38	161	147	14	76	73	3
Ornamental horticulture	200	176	24	10	9	1	2	2	—
Agricultural and farm management	213	210	3	—	—	—	—	—	—
Agricultural economics	1,175	1,165	10	417	403	14	212	209	3
Agricultural business	883	865	18	5	5	—	—	—	—
Food science and technology	333	286	47	188	155	33	119	110	9
Forestry	1,826	1,804	22	291	282	9	92	92	—
Natural resources management	424	396	28	76	74	2	16	16	—
Agriculture and forestry technologies	154	154	—	16	16	—	8	8	—

SOURCE: U.S. Department of Health, Education, and Welfare, National Center for Education Statistics, *Earned Degrees Conferred, 1970-71.*

Appendix A.—Continued

Major field of study	Bachelor's degrees requiring 4 or 5 years			Second level (master's) degrees			Doctor's degrees (Ph.D., Ed.D., etc.)		
	Total	Men	Women	Total	Men	Women	Total	Men	Women
1	2	3	4	5	6	7	8	9	10
Range management	136	134	2	27	27	—	15	15	—
Other	711	681	30	164	147	17	43	42	1
Architecture and environmental design	5,570	4,906	664	1,705	1,469	236	36	33	3
Environmental design, general	568	404	164	58	42	16	2	—	2
Architecture	3,459	3,284	175	625	578	47	6	6	—
Interior design	314	82	232	6	2	4	—	—	—
Landscape architecture	505	474	31	107	99	8	1	1	—
Urban architecture	—	—	—	60	54	6	3	2	1
City, community, and regional planning	229	204	25	810	658	152	23	23	—
Other	495	458	37	39	36	3	1	1	—
Area studies	2,492	1,174	1,318	1,007	618	389	144	120	24
Asian studies, general	162	83	79	100	68	32	6	5	1
East Asian studies	42	18	24	87	65	22	8	7	1
South Asian (India, etc.) studies	26	16	10	18	11	7	3	3	—
Southeast Asian studies	10	5	5	8	6	2	—	—	—
African studies	13	5	8	67	40	27	2	2	—
Islamic studies	3	1	2	—	—	—	1	1	—
Russian and Slavic studies	136	73	63	49	29	20	4	4	—

Latin American studies	280	148	132	148	78	70	3	3	—
Middle Eastern studies	4	2	2	8	6	2	—	—	—
European studies, general	51	31	20	—	—	—	—	—	—
Eastern European studies	20	17	3	—	—	—	—	—	—
West European studies	26	11	15	6	4	2	—	—	18
American studies	1,466	630	836	231	106	125	67	49	—
Pacific area studies	1	1	—	—	—	—	—	—	—
Other	252	133	119	285	205	80	50	46	4
Biological sciences	35,743	25,333	10,410	5,728	3,805	1,923	3,645	3,050	595
Biology, general	26,294	18,253	8,041	2,665	1,746	919	536	405	131
Botany, general	546	349	197	311	212	99	223	195	28
Bacteriology	353	210	143	74	47	27	42	34	8
Plant pathology	15	13	2	90	69	21	105	100	5
Plant physiology	7	6	1	28	19	9	37	34	3
Zoology, general	5,380	4,314	1,066	691	451	240	418	346	72
Pathology, human and animal	—	—	—	65	54	11	68	62	6
Pharmacology, human and animal	1	1	—	75	58	17	161	141	20
Physiology, human and animal	177	145	32	148	116	32	245	204	41
Microbiology	1,122	596	526	382	224	158	323	264	59
Anatomy	5	4	1	112	73	39	149	126	23
Histology	—	—	—	1	1	—	1	1	—
Biochemistry	568	430	138	251	152	99	517	436	81
Biophysics	53	34	19	39	31	8	101	87	14
Molecular biology	66	49	17	6	4	2	32	25	7
Cell biology	29	17	12	6	1	5	15	10	6
Marine biology	52	50	2	45	40	5	12	12	—

SOURCE: U.S. Department of Health, Education, and Welfare, National Center for Education Statistics, *Earned Degrees Conferred: 1970-71.*

Appendix A.—Continued

Major field of study	Bachelor's degrees requiring 4 or 5 years			Second level (master's) degrees			Doctor's degrees (Ph.D., Ed.D., etc.)		
	Total	Men	Women	Total	Men	Women	Total	Men	Women
1	2	3	4	5	6	7	8	9	10
Biometrics and biostatistics	8	4	4	44	31	13	24	20	4
Ecology	96	78	18	21	16	5	17	15	2
Entomology	164	147	17	188	161	27	215	202	13
Genetics	46	22	24	88	51	37	128	109	19
Radiobiology	—	—	—	25	19	6	13	11	2
Nutrition, scientific	38	14	24	103	23	80	42	32	10
Neurosciences	22	16	6	2	2	—	8	7	1
Toxicology	—	—	—	9	4	5	5	4	1
Embryology	—	—	—	—	—	—	1	—	1
Other	701	581	120	259	200	59	206	168	38
Business and management	115,527	105,060	10,467	26,544	25,506	1,038	810	787	23
Business and commerce, general	30,187	27,208	2,979	8,693	8,316	377	190	188	2
Accounting	22,099	20,036	2,063	1,097	994	103	61	58	3
Business statistics	198	171	27	104	97	7	7	7	—
Banking and finance	5,922	5,757	165	1,781	1,741	40	23	23	—
Investments and securities	183	174	9	47	44	3	2	2	—
Business management and administration	28,028	26,096	1,932	9,571	9,253	318	306	296	10
Operations research	136	129	7	504	476	28	50	48	2
Hotel and restaurant management	616	568	48	18	17	1	—	—	—

Marketing and purchasing	15,985	14,696	1,289	1,383	1,325	58	25	25	—
Transportation and public utilities	662	656	6	63	63	—	3	3	—
Real estate	420	404	16	40	40	—	3	3	—
Insurance	478	464	14	18	18	—	3	3	—
International business	220	202	18	245	235	10	6	6	—
Secretarial studies	1,323	34	1,289	—	—	—	—	—	—
Personnel management	1,205	1,116	89	296	288	8	3	3	—
Labor and industrial relations	1,148	1,094	54	300	284	16	25	24	1
Business economics	2,179	2,051	128	242	225	17	66	62	4
Other	4,538	4,204	334	2,142	2,090	52	37	36	1
Communications	10,802	6,989	3,813	1,856	1,214	642	145	126	19
Communications, general	1,734	1,068	666	518	314	204	93	78	15
Journalism	5,144	2,883	2,261	853	558	295	15	13	2
Radio/television	1,899	1,561	338	195	143	52	5	5	—
Advertising	1,194	882	312	94	73	21	—	—	—
Communication media	478	330	148	86	56	30	—	—	—
Other	353	265	88	110	70	40	32	30	2
Computer and information sciences	2,388	2,064	324	1,588	1,424	164	128	125	3
Computer and information sciences, general	1,624	1,388	236	1,131	988	143	110	107	3
Information sciences and systems	177	146	31	143	130	13	11	11	—
Data processing	409	360	49	171	166	5	—	—	—
Computer programing	32	32	—	5	5	—	—	—	—
Systems analysis	88	87	1	88	86	2	6	6	—

SOURCE: U.S. Department of Health, Education, and Welfare, National Center for Education Statistics, *Earned Degrees Conferred 1970-71.*

Appendix A.—Continued

Major field of study	Bachelor's degrees requiring 4 or 5 years			Second level (master's) degrees			Doctor's degrees (Ph.D., Ed.D., etc.)		
	Total	Men	Women	Total	Men	Women	Total	Men	Women
1	2	3	4	5	6	7	8	9	10
Other	58	51	7	50	49	1	1	1	—
Education	176,571	45,089	131,482	88,716	38,899	49,817	6,398	5,043	1,355
Education, general	2,026	383	1,643	12,867	5,458	7,409	1,598	1,272	326
Elementary education, general	90,432	8,090	82,342	17,070	3,123	13,947	219	116	103
Secondary education, general	3,549	1,529	2,020	5,422	2,937	2,485	212	170	42
Junior high school education	721	260	461	134	67	67	2	1	1
Higher education, general	6	6	—	308	145	163	274	233	41
Junior and community college education	1	1	—	91	55	36	6	5	1
Adult and continuing education ..	12	7	5	239	141	98	45	35	10
Special education, general	2,320	341	1,979	3,051	845	2,206	114	77	37
Administration of special education	—	—	—	106	40	66	9	6	3
Education of the mentally retarded	2,640	375	2,265	935	267	668	18	13	5
Education of the gifted	12	1	11	28	7	21	—	—	—
Education of the deaf	239	11	228	208	40	168	4	2	2
Education of the culturally disadvantaged	3	1	2	115	54	61	—	—	—
Education of the visually handicapped ...	78	4	74	97	25	72	2	1	1
Speech correction	2,358	284	2,074	572	78	494	40	30	10
Education of the emotionally disturbed ...	347	56	291	378	91	287	14	9	5

Remedial education	—	—	—	87	17	70	—	—	—
Special learning disabilities	125	9	116	179	37	142	2	2	—
Education of the physically handicapped	149	17	132	150	32	118	—	—	—
Education of the multiply handicapped	63	4	59	50	12	38	—	—	—
Social foundations	180	110	70	534	304	230	129	98	31
Educational psychology	307	198	109	1,286	612	674	362	274	88
Pre-elementary education	3,405	47	3,358	533	34	499	9	2	7
Educational statistics and research	3	—	3	61	34	27	58	45	13
Educational testing, evaluation, and measurement	—	—	—	222	106	116	30	24	6
Student personnel	7	3	4	13,335	6,589	6,746	556	440	116
Educational administration	5	4	1	7,702	6,127	1,575	957	875	82
Educational supervision	—	—	—	707	333	374	71	62	9
Curriculum and instruction	296	81	215	2,261	887	1,374	458	341	117
Reading education	9	1	8	2,789	299	2,490	61	31	30
Art education	5,661	1,598	4,063	998	334	664	53	37	16
Music education	7,264	3,064	4,200	1,564	837	727	109	95	14
Mathematics education	2,217	1,078	1,139	782	429	353	49	34	15
Science education	891	479	412	883	540	343	91	76	15
Physical education	24,732	15,177	9,555	4,410	3,032	1,378	283	214	69
Driver and safety education	132	99	33	171	146	25	2	1	1
Health education	1,089	447	642	405	199	206	51	43	8
Business, commerce and distributive education	8,550	2,627	5,923	1,924	777	1,147	82	56	26
Industrial arts, vocational and technical education	7,071	6,965	106	2,099	1,988	111	106	100	6

SOURCE: U.S. Department of Health, Education, and Welfare, National Center for Education Statistics, *Earned Degrees Conferred: 1970-71.*

Appendix A.—Continued

Major field of study	Bachelor's degrees requiring 4 or 5 years			Second level (master's) degrees			Doctor's degrees (Ph.D, Ed.D, etc.)		
	Total	Men	Women	Total	Men	Women	Total	Men	Women
1	2	3	4	5	6	7	8	9	10
Agricultural education	1,398	1,384	14	447	426	21	43	42	1
Education of exceptional children, not classified above	26	3	23	112	26	86	4	3	1
Home economics education	6,449	94	6,355	802	77	725	28	1	27
Nursing education	603	13	590	330	13	317	28	1	27
Other	1,195	238	957	2,272	1,279	993	219	176	43
Engineering	50,046	49,646	400	16,443	16,258	185	3,638	3,615	23
Engineering, general	2,864	2,829	35	813	804	9	219	216	3
Aerospace, aeronautical, astronautical engineering	2,443	2,426	17	717	711	6	217	214	3
Agricultural engineering	504	503	1	135	134	1	55	55	—
Architectural engineering	272	268	4	31	29	2	3	3	—
Bioengineering and biomedical engineering .	68	67	1	73	72	1	29	29	—
Chemical engineering	3,579	3,516	63	1,100	1,074	26	406	404	2
Petroleum engineering	292	291	1	100	99	1	17	17	—
Civil, construction, and transportation engineering	6,526	6,474	52	2,425	2,397	28	446	443	3
Electrical, electronics, communications engineering	12,198	12,122	76	4,282	4,252	30	879	876	3

Mechanical engineering	8,858	8,817	41	2,237	2,232	5	438	438	—
Geological engineering	123	122	1	39	39	—	9	9	—
Geophysical engineering	26	26	—	7	7	—	1	1	—
Industrial and management engineering	3,171	3,152	19	1,921	1,898	23	139	136	3
Metallurgical engineering	623	617	6	273	272	1	148	147	1
Materials engineering	76	73	3	124	118	6	78	77	1
Ceramic engineering	178	174	4	39	39	—	25	25	—
Textile engineering	212	211	1	32	31	1	1	1	—
Mining and mineral engineering	158	157	1	66	66	—	43	43	1
Engineering physics	373	368	5	65	63	2	26	25	—
Nuclear engineering	250	246	4	329	327	2	120	120	1
Engineering mechanics	260	258	2	264	262	2	148	147	—
Environmental and sanitary engineering	54	52	2	238	224	14	49	49	1
Naval architecture and marine engineering	416	415	1	71	71	—	13	13	—
Ocean engineering	64	64	—	52	52	—	1	1	—
Engineering technologies	5,148	5,106	42	134	134	—	1	1	—
Other	1,310	1,292	18	876	851	25	127	125	2
Fine and applied arts	30,394	12,256	18,138	6,675	3,510	3,165	621	483	138
Fine arts, general	3,595	1,272	2,323	556	268	288	28	21	7
Art	10,688	3,920	6,768	1,690	960	730	6	3	3
Art history and appreciation	1,709	333	1,376	263	92	171	46	24	22
Music (performing, composition, theory)	3,318	1,559	1,759	1,713	878	835	200	164	36
Music (liberal arts program)	2,648	1,124	1,524	623	352	271	86	73	13
Music history and appreciation	96	43	53	99	47	52	40	36	4
Dramatic arts	3,675	1,661	2,014	1,039	549	490	122	100	22

SOURCE: U.S. Department of Health, Education, and Welfare, National Center for Education Statistics, *Earned Degrees Conferred: 1970-71.*

Appendix A.—Continued

Major field of study	Bachelor's degrees requiring 4 or 5 years			Second level (master's) degrees			Doctor's degrees (Ph.D., Ed.D., etc.)		
1	Total 2	Men 3	Women 4	Total 5	Men 6	Women 7	Total 8	Men 9	Women 10
Dance	297	23	274	78	10	68	1	—	1
Applied design	2,048	916	1,132	120	82	38	2	1	1
Cinematography	70	58	12	26	24	2	—	—	—
Photography	477	401	76	57	50	7	—	—	—
Other	1,773	946	827	411	198	213	90	61	29
Foreign languages	19,945	5,075	14,870	4,755	1,642	3,113	781	484	297
Foreign languages, general	607	219	388	444	171	273	122	67	55
French	7,306	1,140	6,166	1,437	331	1,106	192	103	89
German	2,601	962	1,639	690	296	394	144	95	49
Italian	201	55	146	87	28	59	10	5	5
Spanish	7,068	1,807	5,261	1,456	529	927	168	98	70
Russian	715	277	438	110	51	59	14	14	—
Chinese	89	43	46	22	10	12	8	8	—
Japanese	77	26	51	19	3	16	1	—	1
Latin	463	166	297	132	49	83	5	5	—
Greek, classical	104	65	39	21	10	11	18	11	7
Hebrew	203	129	74	19	17	2	4	4	—
Arabic	15	4	11	6	6	—	4	3	1
Indian (Asiatic)	1	1	—	—	—	—	3	3	—

Scandinavian languages	62	16	46	29	13	16	1	1	—
Slavic languages (other than Russian)	110	55	55	88	37	51	32	24	8
African languages (non-Semitic)	2	—	2	3	2	1	1	—	1
Other	321	110	211	192	89	103	54	43	11
Health professions	25,226	5,788	19,438	5,749	2,567	3,182	466	389	77
Health professions, general	230	140	90	46	26	20	12	11	1
Hospital and health care administration	60	56	4	496	436	60	14	14	—
Nursing	12,199	253	11,946	1,530	31	1,499	7	1	6
Dental specialties	5	5	—	450	428	22	14	14	—
Medical specialties	11	11	—	129	106	23	43	29	14
Occupational therapy	663	26	637	51	6	45	—	—	—
Optometry	351	339	12	12	10	2	2	2	—
Pharmacy	4,549	3,636	913	194	154	40	94	93	1
Physical therapy	1,252	257	995	73	19	54	—	—	—
Dental hygiene	531	2	529	24	—	24	—	—	—
Public health	127	91	36	1,244	772	472	85	66	19
Medical record librarianship	148	7	141	—	—	—	—	—	—
Podiatry or podiatric medicine	—	—	—	6	6	—	—	—	—
Biomedical communication	—	—	—	5	5	—	—	—	—
Veterinary medicine specialties	2	2	—	89	83	6	46	45	1
Speech pathology and audiology	1,427	176	1,251	823	152	671	70	48	22
Chiropractic	2	2	—	—	—	—	—	—	—
Clinical social work	36	24	12	304	166	138	7	5	2
Medical laboratory technologies	3,097	386	2,711	45	13	32	4	3	1
Dental technologies	62	62	—	—	—	—	—	—	—

SOURCE: U.S. Department of Health, Education, and Welfare, National Center for Education Statistics, *Earned Degrees Conferred: 1970–71.*

Appendix A.—Continued

Major field of study	Bachelor's degrees requiring 4 or 5 years			Second level (master's) degrees			Doctor's degrees (Ph.D, Ed.D., etc.)		
	Total	Men	Women	Total	Men	Women	Total	Men	Women
1	2	3	4	5	6	7	8	9	10
Radiologic technologies	48	29	19	32	23	9	10	10	—
Other	426	284	142	196	131	65	58	48	10
Home economics	11,167	301	10,866	1,452	88	1,364	123	48	75
Home economics, general	5,439	49	5,390	648	21	627	18	—	18
Home decoration and home equipment . . .	376	17	359	31	—	31	1	—	1
Clothing and textiles	1,521	13	1,508	123	2	121	8	—	8
Consumer economics and home management . . .	232	13	219	58	2	56	5	1	4
Family relations and child development . . .	1,667	41	1,626	296	45	251	55	34	21
Foods and nutrition	981	19	962	231	10	221	33	13	20
Institutional management and cafeteria management	342	128	214	32	6	26	2	—	2
Other	609	21	588	33	2	31	1	—	1
Law	545	518	27	955	909	46	20	20	—
Law, general	536	509	27	922	880	42	20	20	—
Other	9	9	—	33	29	4	—	—	—
Letters	73,122	28,546	44,576	12,710	5,407	7,303	2,416	1,849	567

English, general	51,562	17,002	34,560	7,510	2,852	4,658	1,008	708	300
Literature, English	4,541	1,599	2,942	885	365	520	274	190	84
Comparative literature	428	150	278	245	85	160	96	68	28
Classics	341	177	164	110	51	59	57	49	8
Linguistics	250	83	167	352	173	179	150	113	37
Speech, debate, and forensic science	6,970	2,983	3,987	1,715	700	1,015	235	180	55
Creative writing	154	72	82	185	132	53	6	6	—
Teaching of English as a foreign language	43	5	38	236	78	158	5	2	3
Philosophy	5,785	4,620	1,165	598	449	149	394	358	36
Religious studies	2,361	1,506	855	728	445	283	160	152	8
Other	687	349	338	146	77	69	31	23	8
Library science	1,013	81	932	7,001	1,311	5,690	39	28	11
Library science, general	978	80	898	6,959	1,296	5,663	35	26	9
Other	35	1	34	42	15	27	4	2	2
Mathematics	24,801	15,369	9,432	5,191	3,673	1,518	1,199	1,106	93
Mathematics, general	24,253	14,951	9,302	4,499	3,132	1,367	971	890	81
Statistics, mathematical and theoretical	214	160	54	495	396	99	185	173	12
Applied mathematics	248	201	47	132	115	17	43	43	—
Other	86	57	29	65	30	35	—	—	—
Military sciences	357	356	1	2	2	—	—	—	—
Military sciences (Army)	86	86	—	—	—	—	—	—	—
Naval science (Navy, Marines)	44	44	—	—	—	—	—	—	—

SOURCE: U.S. Department of Health, Education, and Welfare, National Center for Education Statistics, *Earned Degrees Conferred: 1970-71.*

Appendix A.—Continued

Major field of study	Bachelor's degrees requiring 4 or 5 years			Second level (master's) degrees			Doctor's degrees (Ph.D., Ed.D., etc.)		
	Total	Men	Women	Total	Men	Women	Total	Men	Women
1	2	3	4	5	6	7	8	9	10
Aerospace science (Air Force)	22	21	1	2	2	—	—	—	—
Other	205	205	—	—	—	—	—	—	—
Physical sciences	21,412	18,459	2,953	6,367	5,521	846	4,390	4,144	246
Physical sciences, general	985	839	146	297	240	57	29	28	1
Physics, general	5,046	4,708	338	2,174	2,027	147	1,449	1,407	42
Molecular physics	3	3	—	—	—	—	—	—	—
Nuclear physics	22	18	4	14	11	3	33	32	1
Chemistry, general	11,037	9,006	2,031	2,197	1,733	464	1,952	1,798	154
Inorganic chemistry	14	10	4	5	4	1	26	21	5
Organic chemistry	9	7	2	26	14	12	58	53	5
Physical chemistry	1	1	—	14	8	6	46	41	5
Analytical chemistry	—	—	—	2	2	—	11	11	—
Pharmaceutical chemistry	2	2	—	31	26	5	66	62	4
Astronomy	102	94	8	100	88	12	76	69	7
Astrophysics	34	33	1	8	6	2	24	23	1
Atmospheric sciences and meteorology	249	245	4	153	149	4	61	61	—

Geology	2,359	2,097	262	606	544	62	289	279	10
Geochemistry	7	6	1	5	5	—	4	3	1
Geophysics and seismology . .	48	46	2	40	39	1	31	31	—
Earth sciences, general	667	559	108	262	227	35	25	24	1
Paleontology	3	3	—	9	7	2	7	6	1
Oceanography	228	222	6	152	140	12	52	50	2
Metallurgy	39	39	—	44	43	1	30	30	—
Other earth sciences	24	23	1	15	15	—	2	2	—
Other physical sciences . . .	533	498	35	213	193	20	119	113	6
Psychology	37,880	21,029	16,851	4,431	2,783	1,648	1,782	1,355	427
Psychology, general	37,219	20,682	16,537	3,227	2,063	1,164	1,443	1,100	343
Experimental psychology . .	44	44	—	60	44	16	72	57	15
Clinical psychology	24	16	8	191	119	72	133	104	29
Psychology for counseling . .	21	14	7	499	286	213	20	16	4
Social psychology	78	33	45	37	25	12	51	33	18
Psychometrics	—	—	—	7	2	5	2	2	—
Industrial psychology	42	28	14	21	19	2	2	4	1
Developmental psychology . .	8	—	8	24	10	14	5	7	6
Physiological psychology . . .	20	14	6	4	4	—	13	2	2
Other	424	198	226	361	211	150	39	30	9
Public affairs and services	9,220	4,723	4,497	8,260	4,274	3,986	178	135	43

SOURCE: U.S. Department of Health, Education, and Welfare, National Center for Education Statistics, *Earned Degrees Conferred. 1970-71.*

Appendix A.—Continued

Major field of study	Bachelor's degrees requiring 4 or 5 years			Second level (master's) degrees			Doctor's degrees (Ph.D, Ed.D, etc.)		
1	Total	Men	Women	Total	Men	Women	Total	Men	Women
	2	3	4	5	6	7	8	9	10
Community services, general	233	77	156	72	64	8	2	2	—
Public administration	425	372	53	1,406	1,255	151	36	33	3
Parks and recreation management	1,621	1,058	563	218	153	65	2	1	1
Social work and helping services	4,608	1,139	3,469	6,019	2,415	3,604	126	87	39
Law enforcement and corrections	2,045	1,856	189	194	174	20	1	1	—
International public service	88	83	5	63	54	9	1	1	—
Other	200	138	62	288	159	129	10	10	—
Social sciences	155,326	98,145	57,181	16,501	11,798	4,703	3,659	3,152	507
Social sciences, general	21,543	11,753	9,790	2,330	1,522	808	50	38	12
Anthropology	4,384	1,952	2,432	766	429	337	241	178	63
Archaeology	72	34	38	29	11	18	8	4	4
Economics	15,758	13,890	1,868	1,995	1,733	262	721	668	53
History	44,663	29,055	15,608	5,157	3,470	1,687	991	871	120
Geography	4,155	3,291	864	649	528	121	164	147	17
Political science and government	27,482	21,966	5,516	2,318	1,839	479	700	615	85

Sociology	33,263	13,610	19,653	1,808	1,131	677	574	455	119
Criminology	659	508	151	136	116	20	15	12	3
International relations	1,212	850	362	783	660	123	66	58	8
Afro-American (black culture) studies	80	47	33	17	13	4	—	—	—
American Indian cultural studies	2	1	1	1	—	1	—	—	—
Mexican-American cultural studies	8	7	1	7	6	1	—	—	—
Urban studies	371	207	164	236	161	75	—	—	—
Demography	5	3	2	6	4	2	8	5	3
Other	1,669	971	698	263	175	88	121	101	20
Theology	3,744	2,727	1,017	2,710	2,049	661	312	306	6
Theological professions, general	1,891	1,644	247	1,342	1,204	138	249	246	3
Religious music	116	64	52	106	76	30	6	6	—
Biblical languages	24	23	1	18	10	8	—	—	—
Religious education	1,365	722	643	937	551	386	34	31	3
Other	348	274	74	307	208	99	23	23	—
Interdisciplinary studies	13,767	9,824	3,943	1,706	1,106	600	91	77	14
General liberal arts and sciences	5,461	3,880	1,581	549	306	243	11	8	3
Biological and physical sciences	3,897	3,193	704	524	407	117	15	14	1
Humanities and social sciences	2,020	1,091	929	336	184	152	21	14	7
Engineering and other disciplines	178	174	4	24	22	2	17	17	—
Other	2,211	1,486	725	273	187	86	27	24	3

SOURCE: U.S. Department of Health, Education, and Welfare, National Center for Education Statistics, *Earned Degrees Conferred, 1970-71.*

Index

180 Women in Education

Boccaccio—28
Boston Latin School—144
Bronx High School of Science—104
Bryn Mawr College—51
Buel, E. C. B.—43
Burckhardt, Jacob—27
Burton, F.—33
Byzantine Empire—24

California—9
California Standardized Test—69
Canada—19
career counseling—16, 62, 70-73, 151
career goals—62-63
career women—6, 67; in academe—121-27; in business—11, 27; in the professions—6, 11, 27, 47; sex stereotyping—70, 103
Carnegie Commission on the Future of Higher Education—83, 129
Carnegie, Dale—27
Catherine, Empress of Russia—40
Catholics—26, 30, 33-34, 44, 130
Cecisbeo—39
Census Bureau—10, 12
Census 1970—59
Christianity—24, 26, 40
Cicero—47
Civil Rights Act—64, 136, 143
Civil War—46-48, 50, 91, 100
Clarke, Edward H.—51
Clearinghouse on Women's Studies—154
Cleopatra—28
College and University Faculty: A Statistical Description—29
College Entrance Examination Board—69, 156
College Level Examination Program—156
colleges and universities—75-85; academic women—121-32; administrators—55, 58-59, 75, 78-79; admissions—77-79, 137, 140; in American history—46-48, 51-52; athletics—69; coeducational—50; continuing education—150-53; drop-out rates—83; educational opportunities for women—3-4, 9, 11-12; faculty—15, 18-19, 75, 121-27, 130; graduate schools—105, 137, 156; presidents—121; sex discrimination